VOCABULARY
FROM
CLASSICAL ROOTS

D

Norma Fifer ▾ Nancy Flowers

Educators Publishing Service, Inc.
75 Moulton Street
Cambridge, MA 02138-1104

Acknowledgments

Illustrations in *Vocabulary from Classical Roots—D* have been taken from the following sources:

Catchpenny Prints. 163 Popular Engravings from the Eighteenth Century. New York: Dover Publications, Inc., 1970.

1800 Woodcuts by Thomas Bewick and His School. Blanche Cirker, ed. New York: Dover Publications, Inc., 1962.

Food and Drink. A Pictorial Archive from Nineteenth-Century Sources. Selected by Jim Harter. Third revised edition. New York: Dover Publications, Inc., 1983.

Harter's Picture Archive for Collage and Illustration. Jim Harter, ed. New York: Dover Publications, Inc., 1978.

Huber, Richard. *Treasury of Fantastic and Mythological Creatures. 1,087 Renderings from Historic Sources.* New York: Dover Publications, Inc., 1981.

The Illustrator's Handbook. Compiled by Harold H. Hart. New York: Galahad Books, 1978.

Men. A Pictorial Archive from Nineteenth-Century Sources. Selected by Jim Harter. New York: Dover Publications, Inc., 1980.

More Silhouettes. 868 Copyright-Free Illustrations for Artists and Craftsmen. Carol Belanger Grafton, ed. New York: Dover Publications, Inc., 1982.

1,001 Advertising Cuts from the Twenties and Thirties. Compiled and arranged by Leslie Cabarga, Richard Greene, and Marina Cruz. New York: Dover Publications, Inc., 1987.

Rao, Anthony. *The Dinosaur Coloring Book.* New York: Dover Publications, Inc., 1980.

Silhouettes. A Pictorial Archive of Varied Illustrations. Carol Belanger Grafton, ed. New York: Dover Publications, Inc., 1979.

3,800 Early Advertising Cuts. Selected and arranged by Carol Belanger Grafton. New York: Dover Publications, Inc., 1991.

2001 Decorative Cuts and Ornaments. Carol Belanger Grafton, ed. New York: Dover Publications, Inc., 1988.

Victorian Spot Illustrations, Alphabets and Ornaments from Porret's Type Catalog. Carol Belanger Grafton, ed. New York: Dover Publications, Inc., 1982.

Women. A Pictorial Archive from Nineteenth-Century Sources. Selected by Jim Harter. Second revised edition. New York: Dover Publications, Inc., 1982.

Cover photograph by Katharine Klubock

Contents

Preface

Vocabulary from Classical Roots encourages you to look at words as members of families in the way astronomers see stars as parts of constellations. Here you will become acquainted with constellations of words descended from Greek and Latin, visible in families that cluster around such subjects as the human being, kinds of mental activity, and aspects of daily life.

This book can do more than increase your recognition of words; perhaps it will encourage you to study Latin or Greek. More immediately, though, it can remind you that English is a metaphorical language. By returning to the origins of English words you will move closer to knowing how language began: in naming people, things, and concrete actions. So enjoy visualizing the life behind the words you use every day, descendants of Latin and Greek, seeming almost as numerous as stars.

Notes on Using *Vocabulary from Classical Roots*

1. **Latin (L.) and Greek (G.) forms.** Complete sets of these forms help to explain the spelling of their English derivatives. Practice pronouncing these words by following some simple rules.

   To pronounce Latin:
   Every *a* sounds like *ah*, as in *swan*.
   The letter *v* is pronounced like *w*.
   The letter *e* at the end of a word, as in the verb *amare*, should sound like the *e* in *egg*.

   To pronounce Greek:
   As in Latin, *a* sounds like *ah*.
   The diphthong *ei* rhymes with *say*; for example, the verb *agein* rhymes with *rain*.
   Au, as in *autos*, sounds like the *ow* in *owl*, and *os* rhymes with *gross*.

2. **Diacritical marks.** Following every defined word in *Vocabulary from Classical Roots* is the guide to pronunciation, as in (dī ə krĭt´ ĭ kəl). The letter that looks like an upside-down *e* (called a *schwa*) is pronounced like the *a* in *about*. You will find a key to the diacritical marks used in this book on the inside front cover.

3. **Derivation.** Information in brackets after the guide to pronunciation for a word gives further information about the source of that word. For example, after **diacritical** (dī ə krĭt´ ĭ kəl), under *dia* <G. "apart," would appear [*krinein* <G. "to separate"]. Thus, the word *diacritical* is made up of two words that come from Greek and means "separating the parts" and, consequently, "distinguishing."

4. **Familiar Words and Challenge Words.** Listed next to groups of defined words may be one or two sets of words belonging to the same family. You probably already know the Familiar Words in the shaded boxes. Try to figure out the meanings of the Challenge Words, and if you are curious, look them up in a dictionary.

5. **Nota Bene.** *Nota bene* means "note well" and is usually abbreviated to *N.B.* In *Vocabulary from Classical Roots*, NOTA BENE calls your attention informally to other words related to the theme of the lesson.

6. **Exercises.** The exercises help you determine how well you have learned the words in each lesson while also serving as practice for examinations such as the Scholastic Aptitude Test: synonyms and antonyms, analogies, words in context, and sentence completions. Further exercises illustrate words used in sentences, test recognition of roots, and offer writing practice.

PART ONE

Thought and Language

Believing

Directions

1. Each KEY word is listed under a Greek or Latin root. Try to determine how the KEY word and the Familiar Words listed in the margin relate to the meaning of the root.
2. Using the diacritical marks, determine the pronunciation of each KEY word and say it aloud. Refer to the chart on the inside front cover of the book if you need help interpreting the diacritical marks.
3. Learn the definition(s) of each KEY word. Observe how the word is used in the sample sentence(s). Notice that some words have both a concrete and a metaphorical use.
4. Notice whether the KEY word is used as another part of speech or if it has an antonym.
5. Add to your understanding of the KEY words by observing all the additional information given in a lesson: the Latin epigraphs (phrases at the beginning of each lesson), the Challenge Words, and the Nota Bene references.
6. Practice using the words by completing the exercises.

LESSON 1

Crede quod habes, et habes.
Believe that you have it, and you have it.

Key Words		
accredit	credulous	divinity
apotheosis	creed	pantheism
atheist	deify	pantheon
credence	deity	theocracy
creditable	divine	theology

Familiar Words
credential
credibility
credit
discredit
incredible

Challenge Words
credo
miscreant
recreant

CREDO, CREDERE, CREDIDI, CREDITUM <L. "to believe"

1. accredit (ə krĕd´ ĭt) [*ac = ad* <L. "to," "toward"]
tr. v. To authorize; to certify; to believe.

When the Red Cross **accredits** a lifeguard, it certifies that the person has successfully completed a course in water safety.

accreditation, *n*; **accredited**, *adj.*; **accreditor**, *n*.

2. credence (krē´ dəns)
n. Belief; acceptance as true.

In the folk tale "The Boy Who Cried Wolf," the boy has raised so many false alarms that no one gives **credence** to his cries when a wolf really does appear.

3. creditable (krĕd´ ĭ tə bəl)
adj. Deserving praise.

Although most of the women who joined the Union Army's first Nursing Corps had received no formal training, their **creditable** performances during the Civil War established a permanent place for women in military hospitals.

4. credulous (krĕj´ o͞o ləs, krĕd´ yo͞o ləs)
adj. Believing too easily; gullible.

Tom Sawyer hoodwinks his **credulous** Aunt Polly by offering fantastic excuses for his mischievous adventures.

credulity, *n.*
Antonym: **incredulous**

5. creed (krēd)
n. A statement of belief or principle.

In praise of the Mayflower pilgrims, Helen Hunt Jackson wrote, "Find me the men on earth who care / Enough for faith or **creed** today / To seek a barren wilderness / For simple liberty to pray."

Challenge Words
deism
joss

DEUS <L. "god"

6. deify (dē´ ə fy) [*-fy = facere* <L. "to make"]
tr. v. To make a god of.

In order to **deify** themselves and thus gain political power, Egyptian pharaohs claimed descent from Horus, the sun god.

deification, *n.*

7. deity (dē´ ə tē)
n. A god or goddess.

Astarte, the Phoenician **deity** of love and beauty, bears many similarities to the Greek goddess Aphrodite and the Roman goddess Venus.

Familiar Word
divine, *adj.*

DIVINO, DIVINARE, DIVINAVI, DIVINATUM <L. "to foretell"
DIVINUS <L. "divine"

8. divine (dĭv īn´)
tr. v. 1. To foretell by supernatural means.

Many peoples of the polar region seek to cure disease by consulting a shaman, a healer who enters the spirit world to **divine** the cause of illness.

Challenge Words
diva
divine, *n.*

2. To know by intuition or insight.

Without a word my friend **divined** my distress.

divination, *n.*; **diviner**, *n.*

9. divinity (dĭ vĭn´ ə tē)
n. 1. A god or goddess; a divine being.

The Hindu **divinity** Durga is a warrior goddess who, like the Greek goddess Athena, was born fully grown and armed.

2. The state of being divine.

The **divinity** of the Inca kings of ancient South America, who were worshipped as descendants of the sun god, represented the sacredness of the state.

3. The study of Christian theology.

"A lively and lasting sense of filial duty is more effectually impressed on the mind of a son or daughter by reading *King Lear*, than by all the dry volumes of ethics, and **divinity**, that ever were written."—Thomas Jefferson

Familiar Words
monotheism
polytheism

THEOS <G. "god"

10. apotheosis (ə pŏth´ ē ō´ sĭs, ăp´ ə thē´ ə sĭs)
[*apo* <G. "away from"]
n. 1. Making a god of something; deification.

Hawaiian mythology describes how Pele, the goddess of volcanic fire, and her family searched for a pit deep enough to house them all and

Challenge Words
theism
theodicy
theogony
theophany
theosophy

found it at Mt. Kilauea, where they received their **apotheosis** and now express themselves in fiery forms.

2. A glorified ideal; an essence.

For many Britons Queen Victoria was the **apotheosis** of the British Empire, embodying its traditions, values, and power.

apotheosize, *v.*

11. **theocracy** (thē ŏk´ rə sē) [-*cracy* = *kratos* <G. "power"]
n. Government by divine power or priests.

Before its invasion in 1959 by the Chinese, Tibet was a **theocracy** led by the fourteenth Dalai Lama, a monk believed in every successive generation to be the reincarnation of the previous Dalai Lama.

theocratic, *adj.*

12. **theology** (thē ŏl´ ə jē) [*logos* <G. "word," "study"]
n. The study of religion.

Students of Buddhist **theology** must learn Pali, the language into which many teachings of the Buddha were translated.

theologian, *n.*; **theological,** *adj.*

13. **atheist** (ā´ thē ĭst) [*a* <G. "not," "without"]
n. A person who believes there is no god.

Percy Bysshe Shelley was expelled from Oxford University in 1811 for declaring himself an **atheist**.

atheism, *n.*; **atheistic,** *adj.*

14. **pantheism** (păn´ thē ĭz əm) [*pan* <G. "all"]
n. Identifying God with nature; belief in all gods.

Walt Whitman's **pantheism** is evident in the conclusion of "Song of Myself": "I bequeath myself to the dirt to grow from the grass I love. . . ."

pantheist, *n.*; **pantheistic,** *adj.*

15. **pantheon** (păn´ thē ŏn) [*pan* <G. "all"]
n. All the gods of a people or religion. (When capitalized, Pantheon refers to the circular domed temple in Rome built in 27 B.C. and dedicated to all the gods.)

The ancient Greek **pantheon** was composed of gods and goddesses who were brothers and sisters—like Hera, Zeus, and Hestia— or the offspring of these siblings—like Cupid, Athena, and Persephone.

EXERCISE 1A Circle the letter of the best SYNONYM for the word in bold-faced type.

1. a respected **theologian** a. pantheist b. theocrat c. accreditor
   d. student of divinity e. believer in a deity
2. respected their **creed** a. deity b. fundamental beliefs
   c. praise d. customs e. prophecy
3. a(n) **credulous** audience a. skeptical b. faithful c. unbelievable
   d. gullible e. restless
4. witness a(n) **apotheosis** a. sacrifice b. pantheon c. creed
   d. deification e. accreditation
5. an Aztec **divinity** a. monument b. custom c. creed d. deity
   e. religious practice
6. a former **theocracy** a. religious school b. government by priests
   c. basic principle d. divine being e. belief in all gods
7. study the Aztec **pantheon** a. temple b. totality of gods
   c. belief in all gods d. credence e. creed

Circle the letter of the best ANTONYM for the word(s) in bold-faced type.

8. a(n) **creditable** record a. unbelievable b. falsified c. disgraceful
   d. reliable e. consistent
9. a means of **divination** a. staying underwater for long periods
   b. foretelling the future c. becoming a god d. becoming divine
   e. reviewing the past
10. a result of **atheism** a. belief in god b. aggression c. autonomy
    d. nihilism e. disloyalty
11. an **accredited** college a. uncertified b. impoverished
    c. infamous d. unprestigious e. ostentatious
12. to **give credence to** someone a. refuse b. believe c. disrespect
    d. doubt e. condole with
13. become a **deity** a. theologian b. diviner c. criminal
    d. pantheist e. mortal

EXERCISE 1B Circle the letter of the sentence in which the word in bold-faced type is used incorrectly.

1. a. The Romans practiced **divination** by studying the flight of birds.
   b. The Toltec **divination** Quetzalcoatl is represented as a plumed
      serpent.
   c. I **divine** from her manner that she has something to hide.
   d. In the Bible Joseph **divines** the meaning of the Pharaoh's dream,
      predicting seven plentiful years followed by seven years of
      famine.

2. a. In 1957 Althea Gibson **deified** tradition to become the first black tennis player to win the women's championship at Wimbledon, England.

   b. In disguise, Rosalind teases the love-sick Orlando about **deifying** her name by carving it on trees and hanging poems about her in the forest.

   c. Because she passed the difficult tests set by the gods, Psyche was **deified** and brought to live on Mt. Olympus with her lover, Cupid.

   d. Some parents seem to **deify** their children, regarding them as models of perfection.

3. a. Native peoples of the American Northeast shared a **pantheistic** belief in *manitous*, good and bad spirits that inhabited all nature.

   b. The Roman Empire practiced **pantheism** in its acceptance of all the gods of the nations it conquered.

   c. A complete **pantheist**, she excels in sports, academics, and music.

   d. According to Greek **pantheism**, gods lived in fountains, rivers, and pools.

4. a. Although excellent, this private hospital has never been **accredited** by the state.

   b. The crew's incompetent performance on the trip suggests we shouldn't **accredit** its report of bad sailing conditions as the cause of the accident.

   c. The school lost its **accreditation** because of poor instruction and exploitative management.

   d. I **accredit** my success to both luck and determination.

5. a. Christian **divinity** students usually study Hebrew and Greek in order to read both the Old and New Testaments in their original languages.

   b. Dagon, the chief **divinity** of the Philistines, was represented as half human and half fish.

   c. Muslims do not regard Muhammad as a **divinity** but as a mortal man chosen as a prophet by Allah.

   d. Through skillful **divinity** ancient Mayan astronomers were able to predict eclipses of the moon.

EXERCISE 1C

Fill in each blank with the most appropriate word from Lesson 1. Use a word or any of its forms only once.

1. P. T. Barnum supposedly said, "There's a sucker born every minute," to support his view that audiences tend to be

   _____.

2. The _____, the best-preserved temple in Rome, has served as a model for classical architecture.

3. The _____ of most environmental groups might be summed up as "Act now to preserve the future of the planet."

4. The Romans _____ and worshipped many of their emperors, often during their lifetimes.

5. In Hindu _____ a person's fate, or "karma," is regarded as reward or punishment for behavior in a previous existence.

6. For a(n) _____ to function effectively, all citizens of that state must share the same religion.

7. The cave paintings at Lascaux in southwest France suggest that Stone Age artists had a(n) _____ regard for the animal life around them.

8. Listen to all the candidates, but don't give _____ to everything they promise.

9. Although a professed _____ she was married in a church to appease her religious parents.

10. Many aspiring artists of the nineteenth century regarded Paris as the _____ of cultural life.

11. Although their profession was hardly _____, Mary Read and Anne Bonny won renown as pirates.

EXERCISE 1D

Replace the word or phrase in italics with a key word (or any of its forms) from Lesson 1.

The indigenous people of India worshipped (1) *gods* associated with nature such as the sun, earth, and rain (2) *turned into gods*. When these agricultural communities were invaded by northern tribes around 1500 B.C., their nature (3) *gods* [different word from (1)] were replaced by the sky gods of the nomadic, warlike Aryans. These new gods, which closely resembled those of ancient Greece, included a principal father god who ruled over a (4) *group of all the gods and goddesses of the religion* that included gods of fire, of war, of wisdom, and of metal making.

Over the centuries, however, elements of these two religions merged to form the loosely defined religion known to nineteenth-century British colonials as Hinduism. Its essential (5) *doctrine of belief* stresses the reincarnation of the soul, (6) *the existence of divinity in all natural things*, and a desire for liberation from material desires. Brahmins, the highest rank of the Hindu caste system, were the only members of society permitted to serve as priests or to practice (7) *the study of religion* and read the holy texts in Sanskrit—the ancient language whose very sound was (8) *believed to have* spiritual power.

1. _____
2. _____
3. _____
4. _____

5. _____
6. _____
7. _____
8. _____ with

LESSON 2

Sanctus, sanctus, sanctus.
Holy, holy, holy.—Revelation 4:8

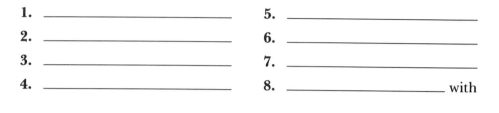

Key Words		
consecrate	impious	sacrosanct
execrate	piety	sanctimonious
expiate	pittance	sanction
hierarchy	sacrament	sanctity
hieroglyphic	sacrilege	sanctuary

Familiar Words
sacred
sacrifice
sacrificial
Sacramento

Challenge Words
desecrate
sacral
sacristan
sacristy

SACER <L. "sacred"

1. **consecrate** (kŏn´ sə krāt) [*con = cum* <L. "with"]
   tr. v. 1. To make or declare something sacred.

   "In a larger sense, we cannot dedicate, we cannot **consecrate**, we cannot hallow this ground. The brave men, living and dead, who struggled here, have **consecrated** it far above our poor power to add or detract."—Abraham Lincoln

   2. To dedicate something to a goal.

   The March of Dimes **consecrates** its resources to research on birth defects.

   consecrated, *adj.*; **consecration**, *n.*; **consecrative**, *adj.*; **consecrator**, *n.*; **consecratory**, *adj.*

2. **execrate** (ĕk´ sĭ krāt) [*ex* <L. "from," "out of"]
   tr. v. To denounce as vile or evil; to curse; to detest.

   Archaeologists **execrate** the destruction of Inca works of art by Spanish conquistadores, who melted priceless gold objects into ingots for easy shipment back to Spain.

   execrable, *adj.*; **execrative**, *adj.*; **execrator**, *n.*; **execratory**, *adj.*

3. sacrament   (săk´ rə mənt)
n. Something considered to have sacred significance.

"Susanna's music / . . . plays / On the clear viol of her memory, / And makes a constant **sacrament** of praise."—Wallace Stevens

sacramental, *adj.*

4. sacrilege   (săk´ rə lĭj)   [*legere* < L. "to gather," "to steal"]
n. Disrespect to something regarded as sacred.

"The existing industrial order tends to recklessness and **sacrilege** in the treatment of natural resources. . . ."—William Temple

sacrilegious, adj.

5. sacrosanct   (săk´ rō săngkt)   [-*sanct* = *sanctus* <L. "holy]
adj. Sacred (often used ironically).

In *Bless Me, Ultima* the Luna family of traditional farmers regards the earth as **sacrosanct**.

| **Challenge Words** |
| sanctum |
| sanctum sanctorum |
| Sanctus |

SANCTUS <L. "holy"

6. sanctimonious   (săngk´ tə mō´ nē əs)
adj. Pretending to be righteous.

I resented his **sanctimonious** allusions to my laziness when he led such a sedentary life himself.

sanctimoniousness, *n.*

7. sanction   (săngk´ shən)
n. 1. Approval; support; permission.

A young person under eighteen must have written parental **sanction** to serve in the military.

2. (usually plural) A penalty for breaking with law or custom.

The senator called for **sanctions** against companies that continued to pollute the Great Lakes.

tr. v. To approve; to encourage.

Before a new medicine can be sold in the United States, the Food and Drug Administration must **sanction** it as safe.

NOTA BENE: The meanings of *sanction* can be confusing. Used as a verb or a singular noun, it has positive connotations, meaning "to approve," such as "The principal *sanctioned* a special school holiday to celebrate our town's centennial," or meaning "approval," such as

"We won the principal's *sanction* for the special school holiday." Used as a plural noun, however, its connotations are negative, meaning "a penalty to force obedience or compliance." Sanctions may be economic, such as a boycott against a firm or country that fails to obey certain requirements. Sanctions may also be social, such as public condemnation or ostracism against an offending person or group. Whatever the method, imposing *sanctions* on something or someone is intended to change policy or behavior.

8. **sanctity** (săngk´ tə tē)
   n. Godliness; holiness.

In "High Flight" John Gillespie Magee, Jr., a nineteen-year-old member of the Royal Canadian Air Force, wrote ". . . with silent, lifting mind I've trod / The high, untrespassed **sanctity** of space, / Put out my hand, and touched the face of God."

9. **sanctuary** (săngk´ choo ĕr ē)
   n. A sacred place; any place of refuge.

During the uprising of peasants the royal family took **sanctuary** in an abbey.

NOTA BENE: The medieval institution of sanctuary allowed a fugitive to take refuge in a church. In some churches the fugitive had to touch a particular object such as the altar, the bishop's throne, or the knocker on the church door to claim the right of sanctuary. After forty days the fugitive could either be prosecuted or forced to leave the country forever.

By the sixteenth century the rise of centralized governments and the Reformation began to erode this ecclesiastical privilege. In England sanctuary was abolished for all crimes in 1723, by which time civil law was sufficiently developed to protect citizens from unjust punishment.

| **Challenge Words** |
| hieratic |
| hierodule |
| hierophant |

HIEROS <G. "holy," "sacred," "supernatural"

10. **hierarchy** (hī´ə rär kē, hī´ rär kē)
    [*-archy* = *arkhein* <G. "to rule"]
    n. A group organized by rank.

In the **hierarchy** of the British nobility, a duke or duchess ranks above a baron or baroness.

hierarchical, *adj.*; **hierarchic**, *adj.*

11. **hieroglyphic** (hīr´ ə glĭf ĭk, hī´rə glĭf´ ĭk)
[-*glyph* <G. *gluphein* "to carve"]
adj. 1. Written with pictures to represent sounds or meanings of words.

Although scholars have deciphered only a few ancient Mayan **hieroglyphic** forms, they can recognize those representing dates: one picture indicates the name of the ruler and another the year of that ruler's reign.

2. Hard to read.

Please type your essays! Your **hieroglyphic** handwriting obscures your good ideas.

hieroglyph, *n.*

PIO, PIARE, PIAVI, PIATUM <L. "to appease," "to purify (with sacred rites)"

12. **expiate** (ĕk´ spē āt) [*ex* <L. "from," "out of"]
tr. v. To make amends for; to atone for.

Since World War II, many Germans have attempted to **expiate** Nazi atrocities against Jews by both public and private support of Israeli institutions.

13. **piety** (pī´ə tē)
n. Religious devotion; great respect toward something, especially parents.

"The Child is father of the Man; / And I could wish my days to be / Bound each to each by natural **piety**."—William Wordsworth

Antonym: **impiety**

14. **impious** (ĭm´ pē əs, ĭm pī´ əs) [*im* = *in* <L. "not"]
adj. Sacrilegious; profane; lacking appropriate reverence or respect.

Many Native Americans regard displays of their ancestors' bones and burial artifacts in museums as an **impious** disturbance and are demanding their return to the earth.

Antonym: **pious**

15. pittance (pĭt´əns)

n. A meager portion of anything, especially an allowance or salary.

Although paid only a **pittance** for a twelve-hour day, agricultural workers flocked to England's nineteenth-century mill towns rather than face starvation on the farm.

EXERCISE 2A   Circle the letter of the best SYNONYM for the word in bold-faced type.

1. such **hieroglyphic** signs   a. carved   b. poetic   c. out-of-date
   d. ossified   e. illegible
2. of great **sanctity**   a. scarcity   b. impiety   c. sanity
   d. sanctimoniousness   e. holiness
3. a(n) **sacrosanct** custom   a. common   b. sacred   c. secret
   d. catholic   e. avant garde
4. to **consecrate** a building   a. deluge   b. enlarge   c. curse
   d. bless   e. excavate
5. a group that is **hierarchic**   a. revolutionary   b. exclusive
   c. organized by rank   d. condemned by others
   e. famous in history
6. such a(n) **sacrilege**   a. error   b. insult   c. act of devotion
   d. act of disrespect   e. creditable act

Circle the letter of the best ANTONYM for the word(s) in bold-faced type.

7. a(n) **impious** act   a. unselfish   b. consecrated   c. pathetic
   d. unexpected   e. sacrilegious
8. offer **a pittance**   a. sympathy   b. a generous amount   c. a share
   d. credence   e. sanctions
9. enact **sanctions** on a country   a. penalties   b. jeopardy
   c. rewards   d. trust   e. war
10. **execrable** behavior   a. creditable   b. sacrilegious   c. vigilant
    d. erratic   e. pedantic
11. a place of **sanctuary**   a. sacrosanction   b. holiness   c. danger
    d. derision   e. circumspection
12. show **piety**   a. credence   b. distrust   c. disrespect
    d. generosity   e. fidelity
13. an act of **expiation**   a. accreditation   b. consecration
    c. credulity   d. desperation   e. revenge

EXERCISE 2B   Circle the letter of the sentence in which the word in bold-faced type is used incorrectly.

1. a. The United Nations imposed **sanctions** against South Africa.
   b. The Pope refused to **sanction** the marriage of Henry VIII and Anne Boleyn.
   c. The goalie's protest to the referee carried the **sanction** of her entire team.
   d. This wildlife **sanction** contains many endangered species of birds.

2. a. Only the Vestal Virgins could enter the **sanctuary** of the Temple of Vesta where they maintained the sacred flame.
   b. England became a **sanctuary** for artistocrats fleeing the Reign of Terror during the French Revolution.
   c. Pursued by an angry mob, Esmerelda took **sanctuary** in the Cathedral of Notre-Dame.
   d. Her **sanctuary** attitude led me to consider her very pious.

3. a. In *The Scarlet Letter* the Reverend Arthur Dimmesdale's **sanctimonious** appearance conceals a secret guilt.
   b. The **sanctimoniousness** of the Indian leader Mahatma Gandhi won him the profound respect of both Hindus and Muslims.
   c. Some politicians **sanctimoniously** attend church only during election campaigns.
   d. Although he himself evaded taxes, he **sanctimoniously** accused those who voted against tax increases of lacking public spirit.

4. a. A **sacrilege** by a priest, a minister, and a rabbi begins every presidential inauguration.
   b. "Comparing Mozart to rock is a **sacrilege**!" she cried.
   c. King Duncan's murder by Macbeth is **sacrilegious** because kings were considered to be divinely appointed.
   d. Because Hindus oppose the taking of animal life, wearing leather shoes or belts in a temple is considered a **sacrilege**.

5. a. I refuse to make my plans a **sacrament** to your ambition.
   b. Baptism, confirmation, and marriage are three principal Christian **sacraments**.
   c. Many religions require that people cover their heads on **sacramental** occasions.
   d. The Hopis considered planting and harvesting **sacramental** acts.

6. a. The new superintendent of schools **consecrated** her energies to improving math and science education in the district.
   b. The great Shinto shrine at Ise is **consecrated** to Amaterasu Omikami, the sun goddess who is considered the ancestor of the Japanese imperial family.
   c. Rather than trust a bank, she **consecrates** her life savings under the bricks of her hearth.
   d. Because of his guilty conscience, Michael Henchard asks not to be buried in **consecrated** ground.

EXERCISE 2C   Fill in each blank with the most appropriate word from Lesson 2. Use a word or any of its forms only once.

  1. Marisa Bellisario rose through the corporate _____ of the Olivetti Corporation of America, starting in 1960 as a systems analyst and becoming the chief executive officer in 1979.

  2. The teachings of Confucius stress _____ toward elder family members living and dead.

  3. Members of Congress regard their right to send free mailings as a _____ privilege.

  4. Jews celebrate Passover with a _____ meal, the Seder.

  5. The lettering on the weathered headstones in the Confederate cemetery had become so _____ that they could be read only with difficulty.

  6. Despite Evelyn Waugh's _____ criticism of modern morals, he delighted in hearing all the latest London scandal.

  7. In Aeschylus' trilogy *The Oresteia*, the goddess Athena helps Orestes _____ his guilt for the murder of his mother.

  8. Because members of the Thai royal family are regarded as sacred, any criticism of them is considered _____.

  9. Although I _____ her racist views, I believe she has a right to express them.

  10. To supplement the _____ they received as salary, rural teachers often had to take room and board with local families.

  11. The "Living Goddess" of Nepal is considered to embody such _____ that her feet are never allowed to touch the earth.

EXERCISE 2D   Replace the word or phrase in italics with a key word (or any of its forms) from Lesson 2.

   The role of women as leaders in some Christian churches is the subject of controversy. When Barbara Harris was ordained a bishop in the Episcopal Church in 1989, she became the first woman to enter the upper (1) *order of rank* in that church. Although officially (2) *approved*, her ordination was (3) *denounced as evil* by many who oppose the entry of women into the leadership of the church. This controversy over the role of women in Christianity has become increasingly vehement during the twentieth century. Although for centuries women in the Roman Catholic Church have (4) *dedicated* their lives to holy service as nuns, only men may conduct mass, the primary (5) *act of sacred significance*. Protestant denominations differ widely in the roles assigned to women. In some churches women serve equally with men, but in others a woman minister would be considered a(n) (6) *impiety*.

1. _____   4. _____

2. _____   5. _____

3. _____   6. _____

REVIEW EXERCISES FOR LESSONS 1 AND 2

1   Circle the letter of the best answer.

1. *deus* : *theos* : :
   a. mortal : immortal
   b. *sacer* : *sanctus*
   c. god : holy
   d. *sanctus* : *hieros*
   e. credulity : incredulity

2. *Divinare* means
   a. "to foretell"   b. "to be sacred"   c. "to be a god"   d. "to defy"
   e. "to deify"

3. *Credere* means the opposite of
   a. "to have cash"   b. "to doubt"   c. "to foretell"   d. "to be unholy"
   e. "to condemn"

4. *sanctus* : unholy : :
   a. *divinus* : mortal
   b. *sacer* : sacred
   c. *deus* : god
   d. *theos* : atheist
   e. unholy : *hieros*

2 Matching: On the line at the left, write the letter of the word that is a synonym.

_____	**1.** deity	A.	apotheosis
_____	**2.** credulity	B.	belief
_____	**3.** impiety	C.	approval
_____	**4.** execration	D.	divinity
_____	**5.** sanctity	E.	sacrilege
_____	**6.** accreditation	F.	gullibility
_____	**7.** deification	G.	detestation
_____	**8.** sanction	H.	holiness
_____	**9.** credence	I.	certification
_____	**10.** expiation	J.	atonement

3 Writing or Discussion Activities

1. Write two sentences for each of the following words to illustrate two different meanings of the word.
    a. sanction   b. consecrate   c. divinity   d. hieroglyphic
2. Many jokes and stories are based on a credulous person's being fooled. In a paragraph relate a situation in which you or someone else credulously believed something that later proved to be false. Use *credulous* or *credulity* in your paragraph.
3. The word *execrate* expresses strong feeling. In a paragraph describe something you execrate. Include some of the reasons for your execration.
4. Most human institutions, from nursery school to the United Nations, have some kind of hierarchy, whether formal or implied. In a paragraph describe the hierarchy of any group with which you are familiar.

LESSONS 3 AND 4

Thinking and Knowing

LESSON 3

Cogito, ergo sum.
I think; therefore I am.—RENÉ DESCARTES

Key Words

agnostic	dogmatic	physiognomy
amnesty	frenetic	prognosis
arraign	heterodox	rationale
criterion	hypocrisy	rationalize
dogma	mnemonic	schizophrenia

Challenge Words
Docetism
doxology

DOKEIN <G. "to appear," "to seem," "to think"
DOXA <G. "opinion," "judgment"

1. **dogma** (dôg´ mə, dŏg´ mə)
   n. A system of doctrines put forward by an authority, especially a church, to be absolute truth.

   The pedantic schoolmaster Mr. Gradgrind adheres to the utilitarian **dogma** that only useful information is worth teaching.

19

2. **dogmatic** (dôg măt´ ĭk, dŏg măt´ ĭk)
adj. 1. Pertaining to dogma.

In traditional Marxism, class conflict is **dogmatic** and is the principal explanation for historical change.

2. Expressed in an authoritative or arrogant manner.

The children of Huxley's *Brave New World* are conditioned by having **dogmatic** statements like "Spending is better than mending" repeated to them while they sleep.

dogmatism, *n.*; **dogmatist**, *n.*; **dogmatize**, *v.*

3. **heterodox** (hĕt´ər ə dŏks)
[*hetero* <G. "other," "another," "different"]
adj. Not in agreement with accepted beliefs; holding unorthodox opinions.

Although the medical establishment once scorned them as radically **heterodox**, Sigmund Freud's ideas about the psyche have become generally accepted today.

heterodoxy, *n.*
Antonym: **orthodox**

GIGNOSKEIN <G. "to know"

Familiar Word
diagnosis

Challenge Words
gnomon
gnosis

4. **agnostic** (ăg nŏs´ tĭk) [*a* <G. "not," "without"]
n. A person who believes nothing can be known about the existence of God.

Unlike the atheist, who does not believe in a god, the **agnostic** simply finds no tangible evidence for belief.

adj. Relating to the belief that the existence of God is unknowable.

Despite her **agnostic** views, she often attends the worship services of many different faiths.

agnosticism, *n.*

5. **physiognomy** (fĭz´ē ŏg´ nə mē, fĭz´ē ŏn´ə mē)
[*physio* = *phusis* <G. "nature" and *gnomon* <G. "one who knows"]
n. The art of judging human character by facial features; facial features when regarded as revealing character.

When he described the Wife of Bath as "gap-toothed," Geoffrey Chaucer implied by her **physiognomy** that she was sensual.

physiognomic, *adj.*; **physiognomical**, *adj*; **physiognomist**, *n.*

6. prognosis (prŏg nō´ sĭs)
[*pro* <G. "before," "for"]
n. A prediction of the outcome of a
disease; any forecast or prediction.

Thanks to modern drugs, the **prognosis** for
sufferers of tuberculosis, once a fatal
disease, is now favorable.

prognostic, *adj.*; **prognosticate**, *v.*; **prognos-
tication**, *n.*

KRINEIN <G. "to separate," "to decide," "to judge"

Familiar Words
crisis
critic

Challenge Words
diacritic
endocrine
exocrine

7. criterion (krī tîr´ē ən; plural **criteria**: krī tîr´ ē ə)
n. A standard, rule, or test on which a decision or judgment can
be made.

According to U.S. law, a person's age, sex, or race cannot be a **criterion**
for being hired for a job.

(*Criteria* can be used only as a plural, as in "Three criteria for college admission are grades, scores, and activities.")

8. hypocrisy (hĭ pŏk´ rə sē) [*hupo* <G. "below," "beneath"]
n. Pretending to have feelings, beliefs, or virtues that one does not
have.

In her novel *The House of Mirth*, Edith Wharton execrates the **hypocrisy**
of "high society," in which a lack of money is a more serious fault than
a lack of morality.

hypocrite, *n.*; **hypocritical**, *adj.*

NOTA BENE: Another classical root, like *krinein* because it carries the
meaning of meditative thinking rather than calculating or knowing,
is the Latin verb *cogitare*, which means "to ponder" or "to reflect
upon." This same sense is carried in the English word *cogitate*, which
means "to ponder carefully and slowly." You might *think* about what
to order at a restaurant or *rationalize* that you need a second dessert
to help you study, but you would *cogitate* about world hunger. *Cogitation* implies that the subject is serious enough to merit this kind of
intense concentration. As the seventeenth-century French mathe-
matician and philosopher René Descartes declares in the epigraph
for this lesson, our cogitation has the gravity to define our existence.

MNEMONIKOS <G. "mindful"

9. amnesty (ăm´ nəs tē) [*a* <G. "not," "without"]
n. A general pardon for offenders, especially for political offenses.

The city council granted **amnesty** for overdue parking tickets to people who paid them by the first of the year.

10. mnemonic (nĭ mŏn´ĭk)
adj. Relating to or assisting the memory.

"Thirty days hath September, April, June, and November" is a **mnemonic** device for remembering the number of days in each month.

n. A device used in remembering.

As a poor speller, I rely upon **mnemonics** like "*i* before e except after c."

PHREN, PHRENOS <G. "heart," "mind," "midriff"

11. frenetic (frə nĕt´ ĭk)
adj. Frantic; frenzied.

Charlie Chaplin's classic comedy *Modern Times* captures the **frenetic** pace of work on assembly lines.

n. A frenzied person.

The once-placid Anna Karenina becomes a **frenetic**, obsessed with jealousy and unable to sleep.

12. schizophrenia (skĭt´ sə frē´ nē ə, skĭt´ sə frĕn´ ē ə)
[*schizo* = *skhizo* <G. "to split"]

n. 1. A severe mental disorder in which a person becomes unable to act or reason in a rational way, often with delusions and withdrawal from relationships.

When Dick Diver, a psychiatrist, marries one of his patients with severe **schizophrenia**, his life begins a downward spiral.

2. A situation of extreme conflict between choices, loyalties, or ways of life.

In her autobiographical novel *Lucy*, Jamaica Kincaid describes the cultural **schizophrenia** of a woman born in the Caribbean but living in North America.

schizophrenic, *adj.*

| **Familiar Words** |
| irrational |
| ratify |
| ratio |
| ration |
| rational |
| rationality |
| reasonable |

| **Challenge Word** |
| ratiocination |

RATIO <L. "reason"
REOR, REORI, RATUM <L. "to calculate," "to think"

13. arraign   (ə rān´)   [*ar* = *ad* <L. "to," "toward"]
tr. v. 1. (legal) To call to court to answer charges.

After officials had **arraigned** Lee Harvey Oswald for the assassination of President John Kennedy, Oswald was himself murdered before he could be charged or tried.

2. To accuse; to charge with wrongdoing.

Legislation protecting Native American rights was passed in 1887 as a result of the fiery lectures of Inshtateamba, daughter of an Omaha chief, who **arraigned** the U.S. Government for its forcible removal of Native Americans from their lands.

arraignment, *n.*

14. rationale   (răsh´ ə năl´)
n. The reasons underlying something, often presented as a statement (used with *for*).

A common nineteenth-century **rationale** for child beating was "spare the rod and spoil the child" because it was thought that children had to have their natural viciousness subdued.

15. rationalize   (răsh´ ən əl īz)
tr. v. To provide a rational basis for something, often by false or self-serving reasoning.

In 1850 the Harvard Medical School **rationalized** its rejection of Harriot K. Hunt saying "no woman of true delicacy" would wish to learn what they taught and they did not wish to be in the company of an immodest woman.

rationalization, *n.*; **rationalizer**, *n.*

EXERCISE 3A

Circle the letter of the best SYNONYM for the word in bold-faced type.

1. a general **amnesty**   a. reputation   b. awareness   c. pardon
d. aptitude   e. condemnation

2. arraigned for one's conduct   a. charged   b. restrained
c. execrated   d. commended   e. apotheosized

3. need a(n) **mnemonic**   a. aid to memory   b. standard of
   judgment   c. means of forgetting   d. amnesty   e. prediction
4. your remarkable **physiognomy**   a. prognosis   b. creed
   c. resemblance   d. facial features   e. physical development
5. suffer from **schizophrenia**   a. persecution   b. severe delusions
   c. rejection   d. execration   e. sanctions
6. explain the **rationale**   a. mystery   b. underlying reasons
   c. overwhelming need   d. plan of action   e. charges

Circle the letter of the best ANTONYM for the word in bold-faced type.

7. their **heterodox** lifestyle   a. radical   b. liberal   c. conventional
   d. weird   e. pantheistic
8. a(n) **dogmatic** style of speaking   a. canine   b. unassertive
   c. aggressive   d. precocious   e. considerate
9. to call **frenetically**   a. calmly   b. sanguinely   c. mellifluously
   d. dogmatically   e. repeatedly
10. a(n) **hypocritical** smile   a. sinister   b. genuine   c. credulous
    d. incredulous   e. sanctimonious
11. a poor **prognosis**   a. self-image   b. profile   c. past record
    d. decision   e. doctrine
12. offer a(n) **rationalization**   a. accreditation   b. lame excuse
    c. sound argument   d. alibi   e. alternative

EXERCISE 3B

Circle the letter of the sentence in which the word in bold-faced type is
used incorrectly.

1. a. "There is no God," said the **agnostic**.
   b. Because of her growing **agnosticism**, she resigned her position as
      chaplain.
   c. Many philosophers of the Enlightenment held **agnostic** views,
      trusting only material evidence of the existence of anything.
   d. Atheists believe they know the truth; **agnostics** always remain in
      doubt.
2. a. Such a **dogmatist** will never make a good diplomat.
   b. In "Mending Wall" Robert Frost is less sure about the need for
      walls than is his **dogmatic** neighbor, who believes that "Good
      fences make good neighbors."
   c. Polonius gave his son a long **dogmatic** as he departed for the
      university, ending with "To thine own self be true."
   d. Most dictators gain control with both military force and persistent
      dogmatism.

3. a. Jane Austen pokes fun at the **hypocrisy** of General Tilney, who abruptly rejects Catherine Morland as a suitable wife for his son when he discovers that she is not wealthy.

b. "A wolf in sheep's clothing" describes a **hypocrite**.

c. Chaucer satirizes the Pardoner, who preaches that money is the root of evil but **hypocritically** cheats and embezzles to get rich.

d. My English teacher is extremely **hypocritical**, finding fault with everything from my spelling to my handwriting.

4. a. Economists use changes in the gross national product and the balance of payments to make their **prognostications**.

b. If you will quit smoking and exercise regularly, the **prognosis** for your recovery is excellent.

c. No **prognosis** in French is possible unless we practice every day.

d. Entranced, the Delphic Oracle **prognosticated** while she sat upon a sacred three-legged stool.

5. a. My grandfather's social **dogma** includes rules such as "a gentleman never takes his coat off" and "a lady never eats on the street."

b. Werner Heisenberg discovered new physical **dogma** about how phenomena behave once they have been observed.

c. Because Anne Hutchinson's preaching on the freedom of the individual conscience contradicted Puritan **dogma**, she was tried for heresy and forced to leave Massachusetts.

d. Personal sacrifice for the collective good is **dogma** in many totalitarian states.

6. a. No **criterion** for success is as important as hard work!

b. Don't judge a child's art by the same **criteria** as those for an adult's.

c. Only one **criteria** seems to count in politics: charisma.

d. You must choose your own **criteria** for selecting a college.

7. a. Because of his **heterodox** political views, the eighteenth-century philosopher Voltaire was forced into exile by the French monarchy.

b. Only a **heterodox** could believe in ghosts and witches.

c. Because of his **heterodox** religious views, John Bunyan, author of *The Pilgrim's Progress*, spent many years in prison.

d. Little **heterodoxy** is permitted by authoritarian governments.

8. a. After a **frenetic** year of campaigning, presidential candidates feel exhausted.

b. One **frenetic** in a class can give everyone the jitters.

c. Trading on the floor of the Chicago Commodities Exchange is usually **frenetic**, with brokers excitedly shouting out orders.

d. A Swiss scientist developed the pseudoscience of **frenetics**— assessing one's character according to the shape of the skull.

9. a. **Arraign** your outbursts, or you will be ejected from the courtroom.

b. Although Harriet Vane was **arraigned** for homicide, charges against her were dropped when Lord Peter Wimsey discovered the true murderer.
c. Reformer Dorothea Dix **arraigned** the government for neglecting its prisons and mental institutions.
d. She was served with a court summons that stated the charges against her and the place and date scheduled for her **arraignment**.

EXERCISE 3C

Fill in each blank with the most appropriate word from Lesson 3.

1. "Spring springs forward and fall falls back" is a _____ device for remembering how to change the clock for daylight saving time.

2. When the new government came to power, it announced a general

_____, releasing all political prisoners.

3. Because of the patient's irrational behavior and inability to

communicate, the illness was diagnosed as _____.

4. Some slaveholders _____ slavery with biblical passages like Noah's curse on his son, "He will be a slave to his brothers."

5. Although for most of his life he was a(n) _____, never certain of what to believe, Ralph Vaughan Williams wrote some of the twentieth century's most inspiring church music.

6. When tennis was introduced in the United States in 1874 by Mary Ewing Outerbridge, men at first rejected the game with the

_____ that it was a "women's sport."

7. According to _____, a square chin indicates stubbornness.

8. The Shahada, which states "There is no god but Allah, and Muhammad is his prophet," sums up the most important doctrines of Islamic _____.

9. One _____ for the presidency of the United States is that the candidate be native born.

EXERCISE 3D

Replace the word or phrase in italics with a key word (or any of its forms) from Lesson 3.

Societies vary greatly in their tolerance of opinions and behavior that are (1) *not in conformity with accepted standards*. Societies that permit a wide range of behavior are termed liberal. Others that are more (2) *authoritative in manner*, demanding close adherence to rules and expectations, are termed conservative. A person may be (3) *accused of misbehavior* in a conservative society for actions that might be readily accepted in a liberal society.

All societies, however, are subject to (4) *offering self-serving excuses for their actions* and (5) *pretending to uphold values in which they do not actually believe*. This contrast between professed standards and accepted practice can produce a kind of moral (6) *conflict between ways of life*, especially for young people who are trying to understand their society's (7) *standards on which decisions can be made*.

1. _____   5. _____

2. _____   6. _____

3. _____   7. _____

4. _____

LESSON 4

Scire ubi aliquid invenire possis, ea demum maxima pars eruditionis est.
To know where you can find a thing is in fact the greatest part of learning.

Key Words		
cognition	impute	putative
cognizant	notorious	repute
compute	plebiscite	sagacious
connoisseur	presage	sage
conscientious	prescience	sapient

Familiar Words
savor
savvy

SAPERE <L. "to taste," "to perceive," "to be sensible or wise"

1. **sapient** (sā´ pē ənt)
   adj. Wise; insightful (often used ironically).

   The word *sophomore*, which means "wise fool" in Greek, is applied to students in their second year of school, a time when they think they are **sapient** but, in fact, don't realize how much they need to learn.

   sapience, *n.*

Challenge Words
Homo sapiens
sapid
sapor
savant

2. sage (sāj)

n. A person, usually elderly, who is honored for wisdom and experience.

Ralph Waldo Emerson's fame as a philosopher won him the epithet "The **Sage** of Concord."

adj. Wise; judicious.

When Wonder Woman presses the star at the center of her tiara, she can get advice from her **sage** mother, Queen Hippolyte.

NOTA BENE: The biological, or taxonomic, designation for modern human beings is *Homo sapiens*. The human genus is *Homo*, which means "man" in Latin, and the human species is *sapiens*, which means "wise" in Latin. Although other now-extinct creatures are also classified in the genus *Homo*, contemporary human beings are the only extant species in that genus.

Besides its biological designation, the term *Homo sapiens* is also used, perhaps with an element of self-congratulation, to distinguish human beings as thinking creatures unlike other organisms.

Familiar Words
acquaint
note
notify
notion
quaint
recognize

NOSCO, NOSCERE, NOVI, NOTUM <L. "to get to know," "to get acquainted with"

3. cognition (kŏg nĭsh´ ən) [*co* = *cum* <L. intensifier]
n. The act of perceiving or knowing.

Researchers in artificial intelligence seek to use the computer to reproduce human **cognition**.

cognitive, *adj.*

Challenge Word
cognoscente

4. cognizant (kŏg´ nə zənt) [*co* = *cum* <L. intensifier]
adj. Aware; having knowledge of something.

Although **cognizant** of the rumors circulating about her favorite, Rasputin, Czarina Alexandra dismissed them as envious slander.

cognizable, *adj.*; **cognizance,** *n.*

5. connoisseur (kŏn´ ə sûr´)
[*con* = *cum* <L. intensifier]
n. An expert or very discriminating person, especially in matters of art and taste.

Museum director and **connoisseur** Adelyn Breeskin organized the first American exhibition of the work of the Impressionist painter Mary Cassatt.

6. **notorious**   (nō tôr′ ē əs, nō tōr′ ē əs)
   adj. Widely and unfavorably known; infamous.

   Cape Hatteras, on the Outer Banks of North Carolina, is **notorious** for the number of shipwrecks that occur there.

   notoriety, *n.*; **notoriousness**, *n.*

PUTO, PUTARE, PUTAVI, PUTATUM
<L. "to settle," "to consider," "to reckon"

Familiar Words
amputate
computer
count
dispute

7. **compute**   (kəm pyo͞ot′)   [*com = cum* <L. "with"]
   tr. v. To determine by mathematics.

   Using a calculator, a student can **compute** square roots quickly.

8. **impute**   (ĭm pyo͞ot′)   [*im = in* <L. "in"]
   tr. v. To attribute or ascribe a quality, especially a fault, to a person.

   His enemies **imputed** many crimes to the philosopher Socrates, including corruption of the youth of Athens by his sacrilegious opinions.

   imputable, *adj.*; **imputation**, *n.*; **imputative**, *adj.*

9. **repute**   (rĭ pyo͞ot′)   [*re* <L. "back," "again"]
   tr. v. To assign a reputation to (usually used with *to be*).

   Finnish is **reputed** to be one of the most difficult languages in the world to learn.

   reputation, *n.*; **repute**, *n.*

10. **putative**   (pyo͞o′ tə tĭv)
    adj. Supposed; reputed.

    Although many others claimed the distinction, Caresse Crosby is the **putative** inventor of the brassiere because she took out the first patent on the undergarment.

Challenge Word
depute

SAGIO, SAGIRE <L. "to perceive acutely or keenly with the senses or mind"

11. **presage**   (prĕs′ ĭj)   [*pre* <L. "before"]
    n. A sign or feeling concerning some future event; omen; foreboding.

    According to folk belief, a goundhog's ability to see its shadow on February 2 is a **presage** of six more weeks of winter weather.

(prĭ sāj´) *tr. v.* To give a sign or warning about the future.

Because a comet was thought to **presage** the birth of a great hero, Shakespeare's Owen Glendower brags that "at my birth . . . heaven was full of fiery shapes."

12. **sagacious**   (sə gā´ shəs)
    adj. Shrewd; having good judgment; perceptive.

Nancy Ward, a principal Cherokee chief who held the title of "Beloved Woman" in the early nineteenth century, repeatedly gave her people this **sagacious** advice: "Work for peace. Never sell the land."

sagacity, *n.*

NOTA BENE: Although *sage, sagacious,* and *sapient* share the general meaning "wise," they differ in subtle ways. *Sage* means "wise in insight and accumulated understanding" while *sagacious* means "shrewd, sharp, or keen." When used sincerely, *sapient* has about the same meaning as *sage*, but *sapient* is often used ironically to describe foolish people who think that they are wise.

<table>
<tr><td>

Familiar Words
conscience
conscious
nice
omniscient
science
subconscious
unconscionable
unconscious

Challenge Words
nescient
scilicet
sciolism
scire facias

</td><td>

SCIO, SCIRE, SCIVI, SCITUM <L. "to know," "to understand"

13. **conscientious**   (kŏn´ shē ĕn´ shəs)   [*con = cum* <L. "with"]
    adj. 1. Guided by one's sense of right and wrong.

Because warfare is against their beliefs, members of the Society of Friends, or Quakers, are considered **conscientious** objectors to military service.

2. Thorough; with careful attention.

Michelangelo's frescos on the ceiling of the Sistine Chapel have been cleaned with **conscientious** concern for their original colors.

NOTA BENE: Don't confuse *conscious*, meaning "aware" or "responsive," with *conscience*, "an understanding of right and wrong." The two words look and sound similar because both derive from *scire*.

14. **plebiscite**   (plĕb´ ə sīt)   [*plebs* <L. "common people"]
    n. A direct vote of all the people of a country or district on an important matter; a referendum.

In a 1987 **plebiscite**, Corazon Aquino became president of the Philippines.

</td></tr>
</table>

15. **prescience** (prē´ shē əns, prĕsh´ ē əns) [*pre* <L. "before"]
    n. Knowledge of events before they occur; foresight; foreknowledge.

    One criterion for a great batter is **prescience** about what the pitcher is going to throw.

    prescient, *adj.*

EXERCISE 4A Circle the letter of the best SYNONYM for the word(s) in bold-faced type.

1. a reputation for **sapience**   a. insolence   b. credulity   c. hypocrisy
   d. heterodoxy   e. wisdom
2. known for **sagacity**   a. good judgment   b. good taste
   c. hypocrisy   d. disgrace   e. sacrilege
3. **cognizant of** the situation   a. afraid of   b. foretelling   c. aware of
   d. responsible for   e. in recognition of
4. her **sage** advice   a. imaginative   b. sagacious   c. pious
   d. sanctimonious   e. needed
5. to **compute** the bill   a. process   b. challenge   c. pay off
   d. change   e. calculate

Circle the letter of the best ANTONYM for the word in bold-faced type.

6. attract **notoriety**   a. notice   b. widespread approval
   c. degradation   d. criticism   e. beneficence
7. a reputed **connoisseur**   a. virtuoso   b. gastronome   c. know-
   nothing   d. expert   e. stranger
8. with great **conscientiousness**   a. carelessness   b. anxiety   c. self-
   consciousness   d. mortification   e. naiveté
9. with **prescience**   a. hindsight   b. cognition   c. heterodoxy
   d. imputations   e. worthlessness
10. the **putative** author   a. hypocritical   b. beloved   c. pious
    d. dogmatic   e. accredited

EXERCISE 4B Circle the letter of the sentence in which the word in bold-faced type is used incorrectly.

1. a. Roman slaves led by Spartacus staged a **plebiscite** against their
      masters.
   b. In a 1971 **plebiscite**, Swiss women finally gained the right to vote.
   c. Voters restored the death penalty in a recent **plebiscite**.
   d. Their petition called for a **plebiscite** on building a nuclear power
      plant.

2. a. During the 1930s few British politicians were fully **cognizant** of the threat posed by Hitler's Germany.

   b. Until I read Willa Cather's novel *My Ántonia*, I was not **cognizant** of the important role played by pioneer women.

   c. Police officers must make sure that people have full **cognizance** of their rights when being arrested.

   d. I can no longer **cognizance** your rudeness.

3. a. She is **reputed** to be the best chef in New Orleans.

   b. At the lower end of town were several saloons and houses of ill **repute**.

   c. Don't **repute** my authority; do as I say.

   d. Until the death of Mao Tse-tung in 1976, Jiang Qing, his fourth wife and the third-ranking leader of the government hierarchy, was **reputed** to be the most powerful woman in China.

4. a. Until I saw her sculptures, I thought Louise Nevelson's **putative** genius was overrated.

   b. After trying every **putative** panacea, he found that rest was the best medicine.

   c. Our visit to the Ozarks confirmed its **putative** charm.

   d. Others may believe you, but I know you to be a **putative** liar.

5. a. Because of a **prescient** need for solitude, I left the party and walked home alone.

   b. Only his **prescient** avoidance of the bridge saved him from death.

   c. With great **prescience** she packed both a flashlight and matches in her knapsack.

   d. Despite his wife's **prescient** dream, Hector insisted on fighting with Achilles and met his death.

6. a. I resent your **imputation** that I can't be trusted.

   b. We **impute** from your resumé that you speak several languages.

   c. According to Bushido, the "Way of the Warrior" followed by Japanese samurai, dying by ritual suicide, or *seppuku*, was preferable to living with the **imputation** of cowardice.

   d. Although **imputed** a half-wit, young Arthur was the only one who could draw the sword Excalibur from the stone.

7. a. A **connoisseur** of opera, my cousin also enjoyed the Grand Ole Op'ry.

   b. Elise Haas, a philanthropist and **connoisseur**, left her collection of twentieth-century art, valued at more than forty million dollars, to the San Francisco Museum of Modern Art.

   c. She is a natural **connoisseur** of the computer, able to invent programs almost effortlessly.

   d. Although this vase looks irregular and rough, **connoisseurs** of Japanese pottery prize it as a fine piece of raku.

8. a. Only after I read the report of the tornado did I have full **cognition** of how narrowly our town escaped disaster.

   b. Alcohol blurred her **cognition** of the other guests' discomfort.

c. Because the **cognition** mechanism misfired, the rocket crashed.

d. Human **cognition** grows most in the first two years of life.

9. a. As evidence that the appearance of ghosts is a **presage** of disaster, Horatio recalls that "the sheeted dead / Did squeak and gibber in the Roman streets" before Julius Caesar's death.

b. In ancient Greece the oracle of the sacred oak grove of Dodona used the rustle of leaves to **presage** the outcome of events.

c. An itchy nose is said to be a **presage** of a kiss from a stranger.

d. Algebra and geometry are necessary **presages** for success in calculus.

EXERCISE 4C Fill in each blank with the most appropriate word from Lesson 4. Use a word or any of its forms only once.

1. The age of a tree can be roughly _____ by counting its rings, indications of the number of its growing seasons.

2. In South America Pablo Neruda is held in high _____ both as a critic and a writer.

3. Portia displays _____ beyond her years when she must decide the case between Shylock, who demands his "pound of flesh," and Bassanio, whose life is at stake.

4. In a 1991 _____, the Lithuanian people declared their wish to be an independent republic separate from what was the Soviet Union.

5. In *Tess of the D'Urbervilles* Thomas Hardy shows that Tess is truly noble, although society _____ her to be a "fallen woman."

6. Our chemistry teacher insists that we be _____ about wearing protective goggles and aprons when we work in the lab.

7. Although they had a highly advanced civilization, the Incas had no _____ of the use of the wheel.

8. According to the traditional verse, "red clouds at morning, sailors take warning," a scarlet sunrise _____ a coming storm.

9. During the gold rush of the 1890s the mining towns of the Alaskan Yukon were _____ for their lawlessness.

10. In "The Scholars" William Butler Yeats mocks the so-called _____ of pedants: they are learned but not wise because they know nothing of life outside their books.

11. Hiawatha often turns for advice to the medicine woman Nokomis, the _____ of their people.

EXERCISE 4D   Replace the word or phrase in italics with a key word (or any of its forms) from Lesson 4.

A(n) (1) *supposed* authority on infants' (2) *ability to perceive,* the "professor" sold parents an apparatus by which they could (3) *calculate* the steady increase of their child's cerebral powers. These powers could, of course, be increased if parents also purchased the charlatan's book, *Genius in the Cradle,* which describes brain-enlarging exercises to be performed daily. Even when his victims became (4) *aware* that police had arrested the "professor" as a(n) (5) *infamous* swindler, many (6) *carefully attentive* parents continued to perform the exercises and measure their children's skulls.

1. _____   4. _____

2. _____   5. _____

3. _____   6. _____

REVIEW EXERCISES FOR LESSONS 3 AND 4

1

Circle the letter of the best answer.

1. *reason : judgment* : :
  a. putative: reputed
  b. prognosis: prediction
  c. ignorant : omniscient
  d. prescience : presence
  e. *ratio : doxa*

2. Which word is *not* derived from the root given?
  a. dogma < *doxa*
  b. frenetic < *phren*
  c. omniscient < *scire*
  d. repute < *ratio*
  e. notify < *noscere*

3. Which word is *not* derived from *scire*?
  a. plebiscite b. conscious c. science d. nice
  e. connoisseur

4. Which word is *not* derived from *gignoskein*?
  a. agnostic b. diagnosis c. prognosis d. schizophrenia
  e. physiognomy

5. Which word is *not* derived from the root given?
a. criterion < *krinein*
b. dogma < *dokein*
c. amnesty < *mnemonikos*
d. putative < *putare*
e. agnostic < *noscere*

2 Matching: On the line at the left, write the letter of the phrase that best matches the way of thinking or acting.

_____ **1.** conscientious objector
_____ **2.** rationalizer
_____ **3.** agnostic
_____ **4.** dogmatist
_____ **5.** schizophrenic
_____ **6.** connoisseur
_____ **7.** hypocrite
_____ **8.** physiognomist
_____ **9.** sage
_____ **10.** frenetic

A. is recognized for wisdom
B. pretends to be virtuous
C. acts in an agitated manner
D. asserts opinions arrogantly
E. decides character by facial features
F. has acute delusions and irrational episodes
G. has discriminating taste
H. finds self-serving reasons for doing something
I. considers God unknowable
J. refuses to join the military on grounds of conscience

3 Writing or Discussion Activities

1. In a few sentences describe a physiognomy that would suit each of the following kinds of persons:
a. an intellectual
b. a precocious child
c. a schizophrenic
d. a connoisseur
e. a sage

2. You are the principal of a school that needs to hire a new faculty member. Explain in a paragraph (1) the criteria you would want a teacher to meet to qualify to teach in your school and (2) why each criterion you mention is important.

3. When you describe opinions or actions as heterodox, you are comparing them to what is orthodox in a community or situation. Think of a belief or deed that could be considered heterodox under one set of circumstances and orthodox under another. Describe the belief or deed and explain the factors that create its heterodoxy or orthodoxy.

LESSONS 5 AND 6

Reading and Writing

LESSON 5

Nomen est omen.
A name is an omen.

Familiar Words
letter
literary
literature

Challenge Words
literalism
literati
transliterate

LITTERA <L. "letter"

1. **alliteration**   (ə lĭt´ə rā´ shən)   [al = ad <L. "to," "toward"]
   n. The occurrence of the same initial sound in several words in succession.

   In "Renascence" Edna St. Vincent Millay uses **alliteration** in the lines, "Before the wild wind's whistling lash / The startled storm clouds reared on high."

   alliterate, *v.*; **alliterative**, *adj.*

2. **literal**   (lĭt´ ər əl)
   adj. 1. In accordance with the explicit or primary meaning of a word or phrase, not its metaphorical meaning.

36

The **literal** meaning of "to spill the beans" does not convey its idiomatic meaning: "to blurt out a secret."

2. Word for word; verbatim.

A court recorder makes **literal** transcriptions of what is said in the courtroom during a trial.

3. Concerned mainly with facts; unimaginative.

The U.S. Geological Survey's **literal** account of the 1989 earthquake that shook the San Francisco Peninsula contrasted sharply with victims' emotional stories.

literalize, *v.*; **literally**, *adv.*

3. **literate**   (lĭt´ ər ĭt)
adj. 1. Able to read and write.

To prevent slaves' becoming **literate** and better able to escape, Southern states passed laws forbidding anyone to teach a slave to read.

2. Knowledgeable; educated.

So **literate** was Elena Cornaro Piscopia, who studied mathematics, philosophy, astronomy, and theology and spoke several languages, that in the seventeenth century the University of Padua awarded her the first university degree ever given to a woman.

literacy, *n.*
Antonym: **illiterate**

4. **obliterate**   (ə blĭt´ ə rāt)   [*ob* <L. "off," "against"]
tr. v. To do away with completely; to wipe out; erase.

Acid rain has begun to **obliterate** the hieroglyphics on Cleopatra's Needle, a monolithic Egyptian monument transported to London.

obliteration, *n.*

<table>
<tr><td>

Familiar Words
describe
inscribe
manuscript
postscript
prescribe
receipt
scribble
scribe
script
scripture

</td></tr>
</table>

SCRIBO, SCRIBERE, SCRIPSI, SCRIPTUM
<L. "to write"

5. **ascribe**   (ə skrīb´)   [*as* = *ad* <L. "to," "toward"]
tr. v. To attribute to a particular cause, source, or origin (used with *to*).

Recent scholarship **ascribes** the roots of Greek culture to African and Middle Eastern sources.

ascription, *n.*

Challenge Words
scriptorium
serif
shrive
superscription

6. circumscribe (sûr kəm skrīb´) [*circum* <L. "around"]
tr. v. 1. To draw a line around; to encircle.

To fortify their camp by night, pioneers **circumscribed** it with their covered wagons.

2. To confine; to limit.

Refusing to let the traditional role of women in the nineteenth century **circumscribe** her life, Alexandra David-Neel studied Buddhism, and disguised as a monk, she traveled extensively in Tibet, which was then closed to all foreigners.

circumscription, *n.*

7. conscription (kən skrĭp´ shən) [*con=cum* <L. "with"]
n. A military draft.

During the American Civil War a wealthy man could avoid **conscription** by hiring a substitute to serve in his place.

conscript, *n.*

8. proscribe (prō skrīb´) [*pro* <L. "before," "for"]
tr. v. 1. To denounce or condemn.

Leaders of the French Revolution **proscribed** the wearing of wigs or powdering of the hair as aristocratic affectations.

2. To prohibit; to forbid.

In an attempt to diminish Kurdish influence, the Turkish government **proscribed** speaking the Kurdish language or playing Kurdish music in public.

proscription, *n.*

9. subscribe (səb scrīb´) [*sub* <L. "under"]
intr. v. 1. To pledge to pay for something or to contribute to something; to place an order by signing.

In order not to miss a single concert next year, we have decided to **subscribe** to the whole season at the symphony.

2. To express consent or agreement; to assent.

Refusing to **subscribe** to the then current opinion that the practice of medicine was among "the honors and duties which, by the order of nature . . . devolve alone upon men," Elizabeth Blackwell earned an M.D. in 1849.

tr.v. To sign one's name to something.

When opening an account, a depositor shall be required to **subscribe** his or her name to the rules and regulations of this bank.

subscriber, *n.*; **subscript**, *n.*; **subscription**, *n.*; **subscriptive**, *adj.*

10. **transcribe**   (trăn skrīb´)
[*trans* <L. "across"]
tr. v. 1. To make a copy of; to write out fully.

Many of the works of Aristotle have survived only because Islamic scholars **transcribed** and preserved them in the libraries of Moorish Spain.

2. To make a sound recording for later reproduction.

In order to study oral literature folklorists have **transcribed** African storytellers reciting epic poems.

3. To arrange music for an instrument different from the one first composed for.

Musicologists who **transcribe** Renaissance music written for early instruments like shawms or crumhorns can only approximate their sounds by using oboes and clarinets.

transcriber, *n.*; **transcript**, *n.*; **transcription**, *n.*

NOTA BENE: A serif (see Challenge Words) is a fine line at right angles to the main line of a letter. Originally a finishing stroke of the chisel employed by Roman stone cutters when cutting inscriptions, this detail was copied by early designers of printing type. For example, the definitions in this book are printed in a typeface with serifs. A typeface that has no serifs is known as *sans serif*, using the French word *sans*, "without." The sample sentences that follow the definitions are printed in a sans serif typeface.

ONOMA <G. "name"

Familiar Words
anonymous
antonym
homonym
patronymic
synonym

11. **acronym**   (ăk´ rə nĭm)   [*akros* <G. "topmost," "extreme"]
n. A word composed of the first letters or parts of a name or series of words.

Laser is an **acronym** for "light amplification by stimulated emission of radiation."

acronymic, *adj.*; **acronymous**, *adj.*

12. onomatopoeia (ŏn´ ə măt´ ə pē´ ə)
[*onomatopoein* <G. "to coin words" < G. *poiein*, "to make"]
n. A word that sounds like the thing it names.

The word *hiccup* is an example of **onomatopoeia** because its sound imitates the thing it names.

onomatopoeic, *adj.*; **onomatopoetic**, *adj.*

13. pseudonym (soo´ də nĭm) [*pseud* <G. *pseudein*, "to lie"]
n. A fictitious name.

Harriet Stratemeyer Adams wrote under several different **pseudonyms**, including "Carolyn Keene," for the Nancy Drew books, and "Laura Lee Hope," for the Bobbsey Twins books.

pseudonymous, *adj.*; **pseudonymousness**, *n.*

NOMEN < L. "name"

14. ignominious (ĭg´ nə mĭn´ ē əs)
[*ig=in* <L. "not"]
adj. Shameful; disgraceful.

In *Henry V*, the French knights boast of victory before the Battle of Agincourt and then meet **ignominious** defeat from the longbows of the small English army.

ignominy, *n.*

15. nomenclature (nō´ mən klā´ chər, nō mĕn´ klə chər)
[*-clature=clare* <L. "to call"]
n. A system of naming, especially in the arts or sciences.

Much of the **nomenclature** of ballet, such as *pas de chat*, a "cat-like jump," or *port de bras*, the "carriage of the arms," is derived from French.

nomenclator, *n.*

NOTA BENE: Scientific and mathematical nomenclature commonly derives from classical roots like *quadriped* or *tetrahedron*. Words for new discoveries or inventions also often take Latin or Greek forms; for example, *wisteria*, named for the American botanist Caspar Wister.

Much of the nomenclature of computer technology is also derived from classical roots; for example, the word *cursor* derives from the Latin verb *currere*, "to run," and *megabites* uses the Greek word *mega*, "great."

LESSONS 5 AND 6: READING AND WRITING

EXERCISE 5A   Circle the letter of the best SYNONYM for the word in bold-faced type.

   1. a willing **conscript**   a. victim   b. draftee   c. donor   d. sacrifice
      e. subscriber
   2. create a(n) **acronym**   a. stage name   b. trade name   c. monogram
      d. name composed of first letters   e. name composed according to
      a system
   3. learn new **nomenclatures**   a. proscriptions   b. subscriptions
      c. ascriptions   d. systems of naming   e. systems of dating
   4. **literate** adults   a. literary   b. graphic   c. factual   d. educated
      e. varied
   5. under a(n) **pseudonym**   a. proscription   b. false impression
      c. alias   d. genuine name   e. exaggerated claim

Circle the letter of the best ANTONYM for the word(s) in bold-faced
type.

   6. public **ignominy**   a. ignorance   b. disgrace   c. glorification
      d. credence   e. execration
   7. **circumscribed** opportunities   a. boundless   b. inherited
      c. limited   d. lost   e. unexpected
   8. a list of **proscribed** books   a. recommended   b. signed
      c. condensed   d. prejudiced   e. condemned
   9. to **subscribe to** a plan   a. dissent from   b. purchase
      c. circumscribe   d. defer to   e. distort
  10. progressive **obliteration**   a. assimilation   b. rationalization
      c. limitation   d. clarification   e. imputation

EXERCISE 5B   Circle the letter of the sentence in which the word in bold-faced type is
used incorrectly.

   1. a. Although your translation from Chinese is accurate, it is too
         literal to express the feeling of Li Ch'ing-chao's poem.
      b. She is too **literal**-minded to appreciate irony.
      c. Don't take me **literally** when I say, "Get lost."
      d. The death of Prince Albert **literally** broke Queen Victoria's heart,
         and she lived in retirement for decades afterward.
   2. a. Although found in Italy, the vase was **ascribed** to the Minoans.
      b. Saying "Happy the nations of the moral North!" Lord Byron
         mocks the stereotyped **ascription** of "loose morals" to people
         "where the climate's sultry."
      c. Medieval physicians **ascribed** insanity, or lunacy, to the influence
         of the moon.
      d. Inside the book, the author had **ascribed** a touching dedication.

3. a. The career of Lillian Gilbreth, an industrial engineer who specialized in time-and-motion studies, was not **circumscribed** by her family of twelve children, immortalized in her son's novel *Cheaper by the Dozen.*

b. In the English folk custom of "beating the bounds," villagers singing and carrying branches **circumscribe** the boundaries of their town each spring.

c. Although the personnel director wished to **circumscribe** the employee's leave of absence and have him return to work part-time, she did not have the authority to do so.

d. We can no longer **circumscribe** to your tardiness.

4. a. Advertising often employs **onomatopoetic** phrases like "Snap, crackle, and pop" to make products more appealing.

b. In "The Rime of the Ancient Mariner" Coleridge uses **onomatopoeia** to describe the crush of iceberg around a ship: "it creaked and growled and roared and howled."

c. *Meow, cackle, purr,* and *chirp* are words for animal sounds that use **onomatopoeia**.

d. Many cartoon characters have **onomatopoetic** names like Bugs Bunny, Porky Pig, and Daffy Duck.

5 a. Many of Bach's organ works have been **transcribed** for orchestra.

b. The Boston Pops concert was **transcribed** for later broadcast.

c. She felt her freedom severely **transcribed** by the rules for residents of the dorm.

d. Clerks like Bob Cratchit in Charles Dickens's *A Christmas Carol* **transcribed** all the records of a business by hand.

6. a. Since the telephone operator spoke no English and I spoke no Chinese, I had to **literate** the entire message.

b. Surprisingly, many very **literate** people cannot spell well.

c. As a culture becomes increasingly **literate**, the art of storytelling declines.

d. Evening programs help adults who cannot read and write to become fully **literate**.

7. a. In Bradbury's *Fahrenheit 451*, book lovers defy the state's **proscription** of reading by memorizing the books they love.

b. Although Uncle Pumblechook **proscribes** gluttony, he helps himself to a second helping of every dish.

c. Despite Nazi **proscription** of listening to the British Broadcasting Company, millions living in occupied countries defied the ban to get uncensored news of Allied progress.

d. If this medicine doesn't help, the doctor can **proscribe** something stronger.

8. a. After the convention, the floor was **alliterated** with banners and posters.

b. Marianne Moore's poem "England" contains this highly **alliterative** line: "Greece with its goats and its gourds."

c. Advertising depends on **alliteration** for memorable phrases.

d. Everyone in the Jones family has an **alliterative** name—John, Jeremy, Jane, and Johanna.

EXERCISE 5C   Fill in each blank with the most appropriate word from Lesson 5.

1. "Around the rocks the wretched rascal ran" is an example of

_____.

2. During the Vietnam War young men with conscientious objections

to military service were not _____ but were permitted to perform alternative national service.

3. In the line "The chainsaw buzzed and rattled in the yard," Robert

Frost employs _____.

4. Children often misunderstand jokes because they take them

_____, not figuratively.

5. Although _____ for centuries to Jacobo

Robusti Tintoretto, *The Portrait of Marco dei Vescovi*, which hangs in the Metropolitan Museum of Art, has been shown to be the work of Marietta Tintoretto, his daughter and collaborator.

6. Agamemnon returns from the Trojan War to meet a(n)

_____ death in the bath at the hands of his wife and her lover.

7. Because Amandine Aurore Lucie Dupin Dudevant wanted her

writing to be seriously considered, she assumed a man's name,

George Sand, as her _____.

8. I heartily _____ to the mayor's proposal to

offer students summer internships at city hall.

9. Henry Reed's ironic poem "Naming of Parts" describes young

conscripts on a beautiful spring day learning the _____ of the rifle.

10. Australian soprano Dame Nellie Melba's 1919 concert in Paris was

_____ for a later recording.

11. A PAC, a(n) _____ for *political action

committee*, is a lobbying group that attempts to influence Congress on particular issues.

12. I must learn to make backup copies of my computer documents: a

power failure last night _____ my entire term paper from the computer!

EXERCISE 5D   Each word in italics can have more than one meaning. Write the meaning
of the word implied by the context of the paragraph.

A. Because Chinese is a highly figurative language, it is nearly impossible
to make a (1) *literal* translation of a poem or even a newspaper article.
Consequently, a poem might be (2) *transcribed* in only twenty Chinese
characters while its English translation might require two paragraphs.

1. _____   2. _____

B. Although the approach road and the several smaller circles of standing
stones that once (3) *circumscribed* the central structure of Stonehenge
have been obliterated by time, archaeologists can trace their positions
precisely in the turf of Salisbury Plain. To preserve such valuable
evidence and protect the Stone Age monoliths from vandalism, entrance to the monument is (4) *proscribed* and the area is (5) *circumscribed*
by a sturdy fence. These restrictions were at first (6) *proscribed* by the
public, but once the rationale was clear, almost all tourists (7) *subscribed*
to the changes.

3. _____   6. _____

4. _____   7. _____

5. _____

LESSON 6

Dum lego, assentior.
While I read, I assent.*—CICERO

	Key Words	
analogy	epigraph	lexicon
apologist	epilogue	lithograph
choreography	eulogy	logistics
eclectic	graffiti	logo
epigram	graphic	topography

---

*An exclamation of Cicero while reading Plato's reasoning on the immortality of the
soul.

Familiar Words
autograph
diagram
grammar
gramophone
graph
graphics
monogram
paragraph
phonograph
program
telegram

Challenge Words
anagram
grapheme
graphite
graphology
holography
iconography
monograph
polygraph
pseudepigraphon

GRAPHEIN <G. "to scratch," "to draw," "to write"
GRAMMA <G. "picture," "letter," "piece of writing"

1. **epigram**   (ĕp´ ĭ grăm)   [*epi* <G. "on"]
   n. A short, witty saying.

   Oscar Wilde is famous for **epigrams** such as "Experience is the name everyone gives to his mistakes."

   epigrammatic, *adj.*; **epigrammatism**, *n.*; **epigrammatize**, *v.*

2. **epigraph**   (ĕp´ i grăf, ĕp´ ĭ gräf)   [*epi* <G. "on"]
   n. An inscription on a monument or building, on a coin, or at the beginning of a book or chapter.

   Every lesson in the *Vocabulary from Classical Roots* series begins with an **epigraph**.

3. **choreography**   (kôr´ ē ŏg´ rə fē)
   [*khoreia* <G. "a dance"]
   n. The art of creating dances.

   Agnes de Mille's innovative **choreography** in *Oklahoma!* introduced the psychological ballet dream sequence to Broadway.

   choreograph, *v.*; **choreographer**, *n.*

4. **graffiti**   (grə fē´ tē; singular **graffito**: grə fē´ tō)
   n. Words or drawings scratched or scribbled on a wall.

   Of all the **graffiti** discovered on the walls of Pompeii, this **graffito** of 79 A.D. is the wittiest: "Everybody writes here on the walls except me"!

5. **graphic**   (grăf´ ĭk)
   adj. 1. Relating to the visual arts like drawing, painting, lettering, or engraving.

   Calligraphy, the craft of writing beautifully, is an important **graphic** art in both Islamic and Japanese culture.

   2. Giving a vivid description.

   Harriet B. Jacob's *Incidents in the Life of a Slave Girl as Written by Herself* gives a **graphic** account of plantation life before the Civil War.

   graphic, *n.*; **graphics**, *n.*

6. **lithograph**   (lĭth´ ə grăf)   [*lithos* <G. "stone"]
   n. A print produced by a printing process in which a smooth surface is treated so that ink will adhere only to the design to be printed.

   A **lithograph** may be made either from a stone or a metal plate.

   lithographer, *n.*; **lithographic**, *adj.*; **lithography**, *n.*

7. **topography**   (tə pŏg´ rə fē)   [*topos* <G. "a place"]
   n. The features of an area, such as its rivers, mountains, and roads.

   A careful study of the **topography** of the proposed site for the school revealed that the adjacent mountain would shade the building by mid-afternoon.

   topographer, *n.*; **topographical**, *adj.*

   NOTA BENE: An interesting word formed from the roots *gramma* and *ana*, Greek for "up," "throughout," or "according to," is *anagram*, a word or phrase created by rearranging the letters of another word or phrase. People have created anagrams throughout the centuries, sometimes in an attempt to disguise a name, sometimes to emphasize a particular aspect of a person or thing. For example, in 1883 supporters of President Chester A. Arthur may have been responsible for converting the letters of his name to the anagram "Truth Searcher." A more complex anagram is "to scan a visible star or moon," an anagram of *astronomical observations*.

Familiar Words
Alexia
dialect
dyslexia

LEXIS <G. "speech," "word," "phrase"

8. **eclectic**   (ĭ klĕk´ tĭk)   [*ec* = *ex* <L. "from," "out of"]
   adj. Consisting of parts selected from various sources.

   The academy's philosophy of teaching was an **eclectic** blend of ideas, ranging from Socrates to Montessori.

   eclectic, *n.*; **eclecticism**, *n.*

Challenge Words
alexia
lexical
lexicographer

9. **lexicon**   (lĕk´ sĭ kŏn)
   n. 1. A specialized dictionary.

   Using a **lexicon** of Homeric Greek, I was able to read *The Iliad* in its original language.

   2. The specialized vocabulary of a particular topic or profession.

   In the **lexicon** of computer specialists, or hackers, the symbol > is known as "greater than," "right angle bracket," "zap," and "gozinta."

Familiar Words
apology
catalog
dialogue
logarithm
logic
monologue

Challenge Words
apologue
Decalogue
doxology
homologous
Logos
neologism
paralogism
syllogism

LOGOS <G. "speech," "word," "reason"

10. analogy   (ə năl′ ə jē)   [*ana* <G. "up"]
n. A comparison between things that are alike in some ways.

In her poem that begins "Because I could not stop for Death—/ He kindly stopped for me—" Emily Dickinson makes an **analogy** between the passing of life and a sedate carriage ride.

analogize, *v.*; **analogous,** *adj.*; **analogue,** *n.*

NOTA BENE: Some analogies are numerical, usually expressed symbolically like 2 : 4 :: 3 : 6. Other analogies, like those found in the review exercises after each chapter of this book, are verbal, though expressed in the same form as numerical analogies, like bark : tree :: fur : cat. Other analogies, often used by teachers, writers, and speakers, are metaphoric. These comparisons are often used to make an abstract idea more concrete and easily understood or to express an emotion more graphically. In a famous analogy, Plato tried to clarify his theory of ideal forms for his students by comparing limited human perceptions to a bound prisoner who can see only flickering shadows on the wall inside a cave.

11. apologist   (ə pŏl′ ə jĭst)   [*apo* <G. "away from"]
n. A person who makes an argument in support of someone or something.

Outraged when her Paiute people were driven from their lands, Sarah Winnemucca became an articulate **apologist** for rights of Native Americans.

12. epilogue   (ĕp′ ə lŏg, ĕp′ ə lôg)   [*epi* <G. "on"]
n. Short concluding section in a literary work.

Rosalind appears in the **epilogue** of *As You Like It* to ask for the audience's applause.

13. logo   (lō′ gō)
n. A symbol or design that serves to identify an organization or institution.

The **logo** of the United Nations is a globe surrounded by palm branches, which represent peace.

14. logistics   (lō jĭs′ tĭks)
n. (used with a singular verb) The organization of supplies and services.

When Napoleon said "An army fights on its stomach," he meant that **logistics** is as important to a battle as the placement of guns.

15. **eulogy** (yoo´ lə jē) [*eu* <G. "good"]
n. A speech or writing in praise of a person or thing, especially honoring the dead.

Tom Sawyer and Huckleberry Finn, who are believed drowned, sneak into their own funerals where they enjoy overhearing their **eulogies**.

eulogist, *n.*; **eulogistic**, *adj.*; **eulogize**, *v.*

EXERCISE 6A   Circle the letter of the best SYNONYM for the word in bold-faced type.

1. the **lexicon** of baseball   a. advertisement   b. graffiti
   c. proscription   d. logistics   e. specialized vocabulary
2. an avant-garde **choreographer**   a. lithographer   b. lexicographer
   c. graphic artist   d. connoisseur   e. composer of dances
3. the Postal Service **logo**   a. symbol   b. motto   c. reputation
   d. specialized vocabulary   e. topography
4. a proscribed **lithograph**   a. dictionary   b. acronym   c. art print
   d. dance routine   e. witty saying
5. famous **epigrams**   a. concluding speeches   b. witty sayings
   c. long, dull statements   d. writings on the wall   e. epitaphs
6. **topographical** features   a. physiognomical   b. mountainous
   c. hierarchical   d. lexical   e. landscape

Circle the letter of the best ANTONYM for the word(s) in bold-faced type.

7. a(n) **apologist for** the war   a. supporter of   b. critic of
   c. parodist of   d. expiation for   e. renegade from
8. a moving **epilogue**   a. letter   b. transcription   c. short saying
   d. argument in opposition   e. prologue
9. an appropriate **epigraph**   a. paragraph   b. postscript
   c. transcript   d. allusion   e. analogy
10. astonishing **eclecticism**   a. literalism   b. analogy   c. confusion
    d. consistency   e. sagacity
11. delivered a **eulogy**   a. speech of execration   b. compliment
    c. lecture   d. sermon   e. transcription

EXERCISE 6B   Circle the letter of the sentence in which the word in bold-faced type is used incorrectly.

1. a. Not a single **graffiti** on the subway mentioned politics.

     b. This new plastic-based paint discourages **graffiti** because neither ink nor paint will stick to it.

     c. The invention of spray paint has inspired great **graffiti**.

     d. She published a book of **graffiti** found in women's restrooms.

2. a. The action of the heart is **analogous** to a pump.

     b. Alexander Pope drew an **analogy** between education and mountain climbing: the higher we go, the more we see still to accomplish.

     c. Using a false **analogy**, the speaker urged the crowd to consider all Swedes liars because he knew one who had been.

     d. After a thorough **analogy** of their over-crowded conditions, the school board adopted split sessions.

3. a. Because of its **graphic** violence, the film was rated X.

     b. With our new computer, we can program beautiful **graphics**.

     c. Book designers need a fine **graphic** appreciation of the overall effect of the typeface, the spacing, the margins, and the paper.

     d. Try to behave politely and **graphically** during our initiation.

4. a. Although the **topography** of Berlin seemed serene, unrest was brewing that would break out in violent rebellion.

     b. Lady Elizabeth Butler often interviewed veterans and visited battlefields in order to depict the **topography** of a battle accurately in her military paintings.

     c. Urban **topography** seems to have steep canyons of concrete cut by swift rivers of traffic.

     d. **Topographers** have created images of all areas of the country.

5. a. This room, which combines both antiques and modern furniture, reveals the owner's **eclectic** tastes.

     b. She claims to be a strict Marxist, but in fact, she holds very **eclectic** views.

     c. As soon as the ballots are counted, a newly **eclectic** president receives Secret Service protection.

     d. They served an **eclectic** menu of soul food, fast food, and health food.

6. a. The long **epigram** after the last act stated the moral significance of the play.

     b. Rochefoucauld delighted and irritated the Court of Louis XIV with his barbed **epigrams** on society.

     c. The **epigrammatic** style of writers like Samuel Johnson was especially admired in the eighteenth century.

     d. One of Dorothy Parker's sarcastic **epigrams** describes an actress who "ran the whole gamut of her emotions from A to B."

7. a. Although outnumbered, the guerrillas had the **logistic** advantage of fighting in their home territory with reinforcements and supplies readily available.

     b. The **logistics** of the Antarctic expedition took more than a year to plan.

c. Because of their efficient highway system and their competent navy, the Romans could administer the **logistics** of a vast empire.

d. Intuition as well as **logistics** is needed to solve most problems in calculus.

8. a. Frances Willard, the college president and social activist whose motto was "Do everything," was a well-known nineteenth-century **apologist** for equal opportunities for women.

b. Despite many **apologists** for Prohibition, Congress repealed the Eighteenth Amendment.

c. The president's spokesperson was a true **apologist**, always taking responsibility for whatever went wrong.

d. **Apologists** for preservation of rain forests point out that hundreds of species of animals and plants may disappear entirely.

9. a. A string quartet played the **eulogy** at her funeral.

b. He was so universally disliked that his family requested no **eulogy** be given at his funeral.

c. In her **eulogy** of the professor, she mentioned her great contribution to both science and the college.

d. In a memorial poem, Ben Jonson **eulogized** Shakespeare's talent but said that he had "small Latin, and less Greek."

EXERCISE 6C   Fill in each blank with the most appropriate word from Lesson 6.

1. So many creative expressions of frustration accumulated on both sides of the Berlin Wall, which symbolized the division of Germany, that a Berlin gallery held a photographic exhibit entitled "Political _____ from the Wall."

2. Lithography is one of the _____ arts.

3. Harper Lee's novel *To Kill a Mockingbird* opens with the _____ "Lawyers, I suppose, were children once."

4. In spite of an international reputation for her revolutionary _____, Martha Graham, who performed until she was 75 years old, thought of herself primarily as a dancer.

5. Although formerly the design of a(n) _____ was cut into stone, today sheet zinc or aluminum is almost always used.

6. A(n) _____ will give the correct pronunciation of the word.

7. At the conclusion of Shakespeare's *A Midsummer Night's Dream,*

Puck's _____ asks the audience to "give me your hands" in applause.

8. The historian made a(n) _____ between Roman civilization and the United States.

9. We have the date and topic for the conference, but we still need to work out the _____.

10. The _____ for the Olympic games is five intersecting rings of different colors, which represent the five continents of the globe.

11. Samuel Taylor Coleridge wrote, "What is an _____? A dwarfish whole, / Its body brevity, and wit its soul."

EXERCISE 6D   Replace the word in italics with a word or phrase that means the same.

A. An opera demands talents that are both highly skilled and highly (1) _eclectic_. Not only does it require singers and instrumentalists, but it also needs the services of a(n) (2) _choreographer_, several (3) _graphic_ artists to design the programs and posters, and perhaps a(n) (4) _logo_ for the production, as well as carpenters and tailors, dancers, and makeup artists. Coordinating all these tasks in the creation of an opera is the director, who must give the production unity of artistry, and the producer, who must insure that all (5) _logistics_ are coordinated.

1. _____   4. _____

2. _____   5. _____

3. _____

Replace the word or phrase in italics with a key word (or any of its forms) from Lesson 6.

B. (6) _Those who argue_ for urban preservation—restoring fine old buildings rather than tearing them down to make way for new ones—fear that all American cities will soon have the same (7) _surface features_, with identical office buildings and shopping centers from Seattle to Miami. They prefer cities to be (8) _composed of mixed parts_ to reflect their individual histories. On the other hand, their opponents, city planners and developers, make (9) _comparisons_ between these old buildings and dinosaurs, which could no longer adapt to a changed environment.

6. _____   8. _____

7. _____   9. _____

REVIEW EXERCISES FOR LESSONS 5 AND 6

1 Circle the letter of the best answer.

1. Which word is *not* derived from *lexis*?
a. eclectic   b. lectern   c. lexicon   d. dyslexia   e. dialect

2. Which word is *not* derived from *littera*?
a. obliteration   b. literate   c. alliterated   d. lithography   e. letter

3. *scribere* : *littera* : :
a. to write : letter
b. letter : book
c. letter : picture
d. to speak : word
e. epigram : epigraph

4. Which is *not* a meaning of *gramma*?
a. picture   b. weight   c. letter   d. something written
e. piece of writing

5. epigraph : epilogue : :
a. alliterative : illiterate
b. beginning : end
c. eulogy : apology
d. *lexis* : *logos*
e. epigram : epic

2 On the line at the left, write the letter of the phrase that illustrates the word.

_____ **1.** graffito

_____ **2.** proscription

_____ **3.** acronym

_____ **4.** onomatopoeia

_____ **5.** analogy

_____ **6.** pseudonym

_____ **7.** transcription

_____ **8.** alliteration

_____ **9.** subscription

_____ **10.** epigraph

A. *Dum lego, assentior.*
B. sonar (*so*und *na*vigation *r*anging)
C. Greek : *onoma* : : Latin : *nomen*
D. a recording made at a live concert
E. Mary Anne Evans wrote as "George Eliot."
F. "the white foam flew, / The furrows followed free"*
G. Oedipus + His Mother (written on a subway wall)
H. Don't speak to strangers!
I. the signers of the Constitution
J. "Cannon to right of them,
Cannon to left of them,
Cannon in front of them
Volley'd and thunder'd."**

_____

*Samuel Taylor Coleridge, "The Rime of the Ancient Mariner."
**Alfred, Lord Tennyson, "The Charge of the Light Brigade."

3 Writing or Discussion Activities

1. Advertising makes frequent use of alliteration to catch the public's attention. For example, a pet food is likely to be named something like "Delicious Doggie Delight" or "Crunchy Canine Carbo-Capsules." Make up imaginative and alliterative names that might enhance the popularity of these items:
   a. a product to obliterate graffiti from walls
   b. a high-tech lectern with electronic gadgets
   c. a device for making graphic inscriptions
   d. a lexicon of proscribed language
   e. a magazine for poor but literate people (with sophisticated content but at a nominal price)

2. Have you ever made the mistake of taking literally what someone said figuratively? In a paragraph relate such an incident that actually occurred or make up a fictional account of such a situation.

3. A writer usually intends an epigraph to emphasize a theme or idea contained in the work it introduces. Select an epigraph from any work you know and explain in a paragraph how the epigraph relates to the writing that follows it.

Speaking

LESSON 7

Dictum factum.
The word is the deed.

Key Words		
affable	edict	interdiction
dictatorial	gloss	jurisdiction
diction	indict	malediction
dictum	indite	polyglot
ditty	ineffable	valediction

Familiar Words
fate
infant
infantry
preface

Challenge Word
fantoccini

FATEOR, FARI, FASSUM <L. "to speak," "to confess," "to admit"

1. **affable** (ăf´ ə bəl) [*af = ad* <L. "to," "toward"]
   adj. Easy to speak to; approachable; polite; friendly.

   His kind and **affable** nature makes Mr. Chips, the schoolmaster of James Hilton's *Good-bye, Mr. Chips,* a beloved institution of Brookfield School.

   affability, *n.*

2. **ineffable** (ĭn ĕf´ ə bəl) [*in* <L. "not"]
   adj. 1. Beyond description; indescribable.

The **ineffable** charm of Diane de Poitiers so conquered the young King Henry II that she virtually ruled France from 1547 until his death in 1559.

2. Not to be uttered; taboo.

Because Orthodox Jews respect the **ineffable** name of the supreme being, they write G-*d* rather than use the complete word.

Familiar Words
addict
addiction
addictive
benediction
condition
contradiction
Dictaphone™
dictate
dictation
dictator
dictatorship
dictionary
ditto
predict
predictable
verdict

Challenge Words
Benedictine
Benedictus
fatidic
juridical
voir dire

DICO, DICERE, DIXI, DICTUM <L. "to say," "to tell"

3. **dictatorial**   (dĭk´ tə tōr´ ē əl)
adj. Domineering; autocratic, like a dictator.

Mrs. Danvers, the **dictatorial** housekeeper of Manderly, intimidates her timid new mistress by comparing her with Rebecca, the glamorous first wife of Paul De Winter.

dictatorialness, *n.*

4. **diction**   (dĭk´ shən)
n. 1. Choice of words in speech or writing.

Use a thesaurus for more variety in your **diction**.

2. A person's manner of uttering or pronouncing words.

During World War II the New York **diction** of Franklin Roosevelt became familiar to Americans through his "Fireside Chats" on national radio.

5. **dictum**   (dĭk´ təm) (plural **dicta**, **dictums**)
n. An authoritative expression of opinion.

"Religion . . . is the opium of the people" is a famous **dictum** of Communist theorist Karl Marx.

6. **ditty**   (dĭt´ ē)
n. A simple song.

Most kindergartners learn the **ditty** "The Eensy Weensy Spider."

7. **edict**   (ē´ dĭkt)   [*e* <L. "from"]
n. A decree or proclamation issued by an authority.

In Orwell's *Animal Farm* the pigs change their original **edict**, "All animals are equal," by adding "but some animals are more equal than others."

8. **indict**   (ĭn dīt´)   [*in* <L. "in"]
   tr. v. 1. (*legal*) To issue a formal charge of a crime.

   The judge who arraigned and **indicted** Grace Newton for cattle rustling was so offended by her profane language that he adjourned the case "until such time as she can testify like a lady."

   2. To accuse.

   The environmental study **indicted** the company for many instances of pollution.

   indictment, *n.*

9. **indite**   (ĭn dīt´)   [*in* <L. "in"]
   tr. v. To write; to compose.

   Although Margery Kempe **indited** her life story, the oldest autobiography in English, in the fourteenth century, it was only discovered and printed in 1934.

   NOTA BENE: Although their meanings are quite different, many students mix up the homonyms *indict* and *indite*. Others misuse *indite* as a simple synonym for "to write." The connotation of *indite* is "to choose the content carefully." You *write* a postcard or a grocery list, but you *indite* the inscription in a book or a toast for a banquet.

   The legal distinction between *indict* and *arraign* can be confusing. If legal authorities think that reasonable grounds exist (remember the root of *arraign* is *ratio*, "reason"!) to believe that someone committed a crime, they can *arraign* that person. Arraignment means the accused person must come to court to answer charges. However, someone is *indicted* only when the court finds the charges for which he or she was arraigned to be credible.

10. **interdiction**   (ĭn´tər dĭk´ shən)   [*inter-* <L. "between"]
    n. A prohibition; the act of forbidding.

    Following the Russian Revolution the Supreme Soviet issued an **interdiction** against the use of noble titles, declaring that all citizens should be addressed as *tovarisch*, or "comrade."

    interdict, *v.*; **interdictive**, *adj.*; **interdictor**, *n.*

11. **jurisdiction**   (joor´ əs dĭk´ shən)   [*juris=jus* <L. "law"]
    n. 1. Control and authority, especially to interpret and exercise the law.

The governing council of each New Mexican pueblo has full **jurisdiction** over its people and lands.

2. The specific area of someone's or something's control or authority.

National parks and monuments are under the **jurisdiction** of the Department of the Interior, but state parks are cared for by individual states.

jurisdictional, *adj.*

12. **malediction** (măl´ ə dĭk´ shən) [*malus* <L. "bad"]
n. A curse.

In Shakespeare's *Romeo and Juliet*, Mercutio dies uttering the **malediction**, "A plague o' both your houses."

Antonym: **benediction**

13. **valediction** (văl´ ə dĭk´ shən)
[*vale* <L. "farewell"]
n. A bidding farewell; a leave-taking; a farewell speech.

In his famous **valediction** to military service, General Douglas MacArthur referred to a British Army war song when he said, "Old soldiers never die, they just fade away."

valedictorian, *n.*; **valedictory**, *adj.*

NOTA BENE: Although they come from the same root and refer to authority, *edict* and *dictum* are used very differently. An edict is a formal ruling made by a court, government, or person in charge and has the connotation of "laying down the law." If a school principal banned smoking on campus, that interdiction would have the force of an edict. A dictum, on the other hand, is an opinion and is only as authoritative as the person who expresses it. If a monarch or a dictator delivers a dictum such as "I believe complainers are unpatriotic," that opinion may indeed carry the force of law, but the dicta of an isolated radical philosopher might have no impact at all.

Familiar Word
glossary

GLOSSA, GLOTTA <G. "tongue," "language"

14. **gloss** (glôs, glŏs)
n. An explanation of a difficult expression in a text.

Because readers found the allusions in "The Waste Land" so obscure, T.S. Eliot provided a **gloss** to accompany his poem.

Challenge Words
glossal
glossolalia
glottal
glottis

tr. v. (with *over*) To explain away.

In promoting its "all-new" soap powder, the company **glossed** over the fact that the previous formula had caused rashes and skin irritations.

15. **polyglot** (pŏl´ ē glŏt) [*poly* <G. "many"]
n. A person who knows several languages well.

Although she never went to school, Mary Antisarlook was a **polyglot**, whose fluent Russian, English, and Eskimo enabled her to facilitate importing reindeer from Siberia to Alaska during the nineteenth century.

EXERCISE 7A   Circle the letter of the best SYNONYM for the word in bold-faced type.

1. a well-known **dictum**   a. authoritative ruler   b. authoritative opinion   c. authoritative decision   d. joke   e. injustice
2. beyond my **jurisdiction**   a. experience   b. area of expertise c. area of authority   d. abilities   e. length of sentence
3. employ a **polyglot**   a. lexicon   b. pantheist   c. person with many connections   d. person who knows many languages   e. person with many talents
4. write a(n) **ditty**   a. edict   b. epistle   c. rationale   d. little song e. dogmatic essay
5. issue a(n) **edict**   a. judgment   b. decree   c. apology d. malediction   e. dictum
6. **valedictory** remarks   a. welcoming   b. condemning   c. farewell d. preclusive   e. affable

Circle the letter of the best ANTONYM for the word(s) in bold-faced type.

7. to **interdict** the demonstration   a. encourage   b. forbid c. interfere with   d. preempt   e. patronize
8. a sanctimonious **malediction**   a. oath   b. benediction c. potion   d. curse   e. outcry
9. **indicted for** cheating   a. accused of   b. found innocent of c. suspected of   e. proscribed for   e. endorsed for
10. govern **dictatorially**   a. implicitly   b. introspectively   c. passively d. sanctimoniously   e. hypocritically
11. a(n) **ineffable** experience   a. nominal   b. readily forgotten c. easily described   d. proscribed   e. expensive
12. **gloss over** the problem   a. confront   b. obscure   c. solve d. impute   e. execrate
13. smile **affably**   a. greedily   b. frenetically   c. graphically d. sagaciously   e. menacingly

EXERCISE 7B   Circle the letter of the sentence in which the word in bold-faced type is used incorrectly.

1. a. My mother's **dicta** are always preceded by "I know you won't agree with me, but. . . ."
   b. "Where are the snows of yesteryear?" is a famous **dictum** of François Villon.
   c. Skirt lengths vary according to the **dicta** of fashion.
   d. Ignoring family **dictums**, Maggie Tulliver befriended her father's enemy.

2. a. Keats **indited** his sonnet "On First Looking into Chapman's Homer" in a single evening.
   b. Each friend **indited** a verse in the other's yearbook.
   c. You have been **indited** by your own greed.
   d. Without your inspiration, I cannot **indite** but only write.

3. a. Because the names of the gods are considered **ineffable** in many cultures, people use only nicknames when they refer to them.
   b. Rudolph Valentino held an **ineffable** attraction for thousands of fans.
   c. The accident left the victim **ineffable**, able to communicate only by writing.
   d. The Andes left an **ineffable** impression on us, one that lasted the rest of our lives.

4. a. Let your coach **diction** you about the changes in rules.
   b. Because of nationwide radio and television, the **diction** of Americans is more homogeneous than it used to be.
   c. Thomas Hardy's **diction** contains many Latinate words.
   d. Her **diction** includes many phrases like "I'm fixin' to go" and "you shouldn't ought to," that reveal her Southern roots.

5. a. Although I felt **valedictory** my first week at camp, I soon got over my homesickness.
   b. At her retirement banquet, Rosa gave a **valedictory** speech in which she recalled her early days with the union.
   c. Many tearful **valedictions** were made in Grand Central Terminal as troops departed for the war.
   d. The **valedictorian** challenged the graduating class to find work that was both personally satisfying and socially beneficial.

6. a. Although written in the fifteenth century, Lady Paston's letters describing how she is managing the family estate need almost no **glosses** to be understood by modern readers.
   b. *The Annotated Alice* **glosses** the possible hidden meanings of seemingly simple passages in *Alice in Wonderland*.
   c. The eulogy **glossed** over the fact that she was reputed to have made her fortune ignominiously.
   d. **Gloss** your teeth well every day.

7. a. The safety commission's report contained a strong **indictment** of the airline's irresponsible actions.
   b. Some scholars believe that Shakespeare **indicted** this newly-discovered poem.
   c. She was acquitted of the murder charge but **indicted**, tried, and found guilty of forgery.
   d. After hearing testimony for three days, the grand jury **indicted** the tearful suspect for assault.

EXERCISE 7C   Fill in each blank with the most appropriate word from Lesson 7. Use a word or any of its forms only once.

1. The director, although pleasant to everyone, is not naturally

   _____.

2. Gretchen sang an old seafaring _____ as she spun.

3. In the medieval investiture controversy both the pope and the

   kings claimed _____ over the appointment of bishops.

4. Bernada Alba utters terrible _____against her daughters when they refuse to respect her.

5. During the nineteenth century the Bureau of Indian Affairs

   enforced a(n) _____ policy proscribing the use of native languages at school.

6. The poet laureate, the official chief poet of England, is expected to

   _____ poems celebrating great national occasions.

7. Although teenage slang is acceptable in speech, more formal

   _____ is expected in writing.

8. A(n) _____ from the fire department warns against open fires during the dry season.

9. Because their country has three official languages, French,

   German, and Italian, most Swiss are _____.

10. Defying the government's _____ of public meetings, thousands of Czechs gathered in Wencelas Square to demand reforms.

EXERCISE 7D Each word in italics can have more than one meaning. Write the meaning of the word implied by the context of the paragraph.

A. Although I delight in the (1) *ineffable* beauty of Chinese poetry, the (2) *diction* is so difficult that even a polyglot like me needs an edition with a(n) (3) *gloss* for the difficult passages.

1. _____   3. _____

2. _____

Replace the word in italics with a word or phrase that means the same.

B. At most schools and colleges, graduation is surrounded with long-established traditions. Almost every American graduation ceremony includes a(n) (4) *valedictory* speech (5) *indited* by the most outstanding scholar of the senior class; an address by some well-known person who offers (6) *dicta* on how to achieve future success; and the presentation of diplomas by the principal, who greets each graduate with a(n) (7) *affable* handshake. Finally the senior class sings the school song, and despite strict (8) *interdictions* throws its mortarboards into the air with a shout.

4. _____   7. _____

5. _____   8. _____

6. _____

LESSON 8

Verbum sat sapienti.
A word to a wise person is enough.

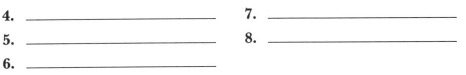

Key Words		
acclamation	forensic	locution
circumlocution	forum	loquacious
clamor	lingo	proverbial
colloquium	lingua franca	verbatim
declaim	linguist	verbose

CLAMO, CLAMARE, CLAMAVI, CLAMATUM <L. "to cry out," "to shout"

1. **acclamation** (ăk lə´ mā´ shən) [ac=ad <L. "to," "toward"]
   n. 1. Applause; enthusiastic approval.

   Congressional **acclamation** for Representative Shirley Chisholm's bill to extend the minimum wage to domestic workers came after months of negotiation.

   2. An oral vote, especially an enthusiastic vote of approval.

   According to *Robert's Rules of Order*, when a group is in obvious agreement, they may vote by **acclamation**, simply speaking "aye" or "nay," rather than by a formal ballot.

   acclaim, *v*.; **acclaim**, *n*.; **acclaimer**, *n*.

2. **clamor** (klăm´ ər)
   n. A loud outcry, especially in protest.

   "Not in the **clamor** of the crowded street,
   Not in the shouts and plaudits of the throng,
   But, in ourselves, are triumph and defeat."
   —Henry Wadsworth Longfellow

   intr. v. To insist or exclaim noisily.

   After Marlene Dietrich appeared in a trouser suit in a 1933 film, women **clamored** to wear pants, a fashion that has persisted for more than half a century.

   clamorous, *adj.*

3. **declaim** (dĭ klām´) [de <L. "away from"]
   tr. and *intr. v.* To speak loudly or passionately.

   The music critic noted approvingly that the narrator for Copland's *A Lincoln Portrait* spoke the words naturally and didn't **declaim** them in a theatrical manner.

   declamation, *n*.; **declamatory**, *adj.*

FORUM <L. "forum," "place out of doors"

4. **forensic** (fə rĕn´ sĭk)
   adj. Referring to legal proceedings or formal debate or rhetoric.

   A specialist in **forensic** medicine testified that a postmortem examination revealed that the victim had died from a rare poison.

n. **forensics** The study or practice of formal debate (used with a singular verb).

Benazir Bhutto, former president of Pakistan, excelled in **forensics** at Oxford University's famous debating society, The Oxford Union.

5. **forum** (fôr´ əm, fōr´ əm) (plural **forums** or **fora**)
n. 1. The central square or marketplace of a Roman city. (When capitalized, *Forum* refers specifically to the Forum in ancient Rome.)

In the **forum** of almost every city of the Roman Empire stood a statue of the reigning Caesar.

2. A public meeting or any situation for open discussion.

Radio and television call-in shows provide a **forum** for opinion on contemporary issues.

NOTA BENE: The Greeks considered forensic ability to be an essential of democracy. Forensics was a part of every noble youth's education, and forensic competitions were among the events at every session of the Olympic Games.
   The word *stentorian*, which describes an extremely loud voice, derives from the name Stentor, a loud-voiced herald in the Greek epic *The Odyssey*. Another famous Greek speaker, the historic orator Demosthenes, is not recalled in any English word, but many college debating organizations are named Demosthenian societies in his honor.

Familiar Words
bilingual
linguine
linguistic
linguistics

Challenge Words
lingual
lingulate

LINGUA <L. "speech," "language," "tongue"

6. **lingo** (lĭng´ gō)
n. Unfamiliar language; a dialect or special jargon.

In Anthony Burgess's *A Clockwork Orange* the citizens of a future society speak a **lingo** that contains words derived from Russian such as *chelloveck*, meaning "person," and *govoreet*, meaning "to talk."

7. **lingua franca** (lĭng´ gwə frăng´ kə)
[*lingua franca* < Italian "the Frankish tongue"]
n. A language used by people who do not speak a common tongue; usually combines aspects of different languages; also called *pidgin*.

Pidgin English is a **lingua franca** based on English that is used as a trading language throughout Southeast Asia.

8. linguist   (lĭng´ gwĭst)

n. 1. A person who speaks several languages; a polyglot.

Although not naturally skilled in foreign languages, she became an impressive **linguist** after living in different countries for many years.

2. A person who studies linguistics, the structure of human speech.

Many **linguists** seek to understand the development of language families, like the Indo-European group to which both English and Latin belong.

NOTA BENE: Whereas a *bilingual* person knows two languages well, a *polyglot* or a *linguist* knows several languages. Both *polyglot* and *linguist* derive from roots meaning "tongue."

LOQUOR, LOQUI, LOCUTUM <L. "to speak"

<table>
<tr><td>

Familiar Words
colloquial
eloquent

</td></tr>
</table>

<table>
<tr><td>

Challenge Words
colloquy
elocution
grandiloquent
interlocutor
magniloquent
obloquy

</td></tr>
</table>

9. circumlocution   (sûr´ kəm lō kyōō´ shən)   [*circum* <L. "around"]
n. 1. The use of many words when few would do.

Instead of a **circumlocution** like "The medical profession disapproves of the use of tobacco by young people," just say "Doctors think kids shouldn't smoke."

2. Evasive talk; roundabout expression.

Rather than acknowledge that the student had been expelled, the principal used **circumlocutions** like "permanently withdrawn from attendance" and "severed association with the school."

circumlocutory, *adj.*

10. colloquium   (kə lō´ kwē əm)
(plural **colloquiums, colloquia**)
[*col* = *cum* <L. "with"]
n. A meeting for discussion, especially in an academic setting.

Ecologists and government officials attended a **colloquium** on global warming.

11. locution   (lō kyōō´ shən)
n. A word or expression; phraseology.

A typical eighteenth-century letter might end with an ornate **locution** such as "Madam, I have the honor to remain your most faithful servant."

12. loquacious   (lō kwā´ shəs)
adj. Very talkative.

The **loquacious** messenger in *Oedipus Rex* brings good news but talks so much that he unintentionally delivers bad news as well.

loquaciousness, *n.*; **loquacity**, *n.*

Familiar Words
adverb
proverb
verb

Challenge Words
verbiage
verbicide
verbify

VERBUM <L. "word"

13. proverbial (prə vûr´ bē əl) [*pro* <L. "before," "for"]
adj. 1. Of or like a wise or witty folksaying.

Following the **proverbial** wisdom that "a bird in the hand is worth two in the bush," many forty-niners gave up their dreams of gold and settled in the rich Central Valley of California.

2. Well-known; notorious; frequently spoken of.

Our class has entered the **proverbial** "senior slump," just marking time until graduation.

proverb, *n.*

14. verbatim (vûr bā´ tĭm)
adj. Word for word; in exactly the same words.

The Congressional Record contains **verbatim** accounts of legislative sessions.

15. verbose (vər bōs´)
adj. Wordy; using excessive words.

To excel at forensics, you must not be **verbose** or you will lose your audience's attention.

verbosity, *n.*

NOTA BENE: Although close in meaning, *verbose* differs from *loquacious*. As its root *verbum*, "word," suggests, *verbose* means too many words, whether written or spoken. *Loquacious*, on the other hand, refers exclusively to speech.

EXERCISE 8A

Circle the letter of the best SYNONYM for the word(s) in bold-faced type.

1. the unfamiliar **lingo**   a. customs   b. dialect   c. creed
d. forensics   e. cuisine
2. the sanctimonious **locution**   a. phraseology   b. conversation
c. edict   d. lithograph   e. dialect

3. hold a public **colloquium**   a. conversation   b. position of authority   c. forum   d. class   e. office
4. the **proverbial** bad penny   a. commonly spoken of   b. polyglot c. glossy   d. little-known   e. traditional
5. use the local **lingua franca**   a. lingo   b. slang   c. pidgin d. French dialect   e. custom
6. seeking a(n) **forum**   a. marketplace of Rome   b. talk show c. opportunity for discussion   d. formal debate   e. listener
7. habitual **verbosity**   a. long-windedness   b. brevity of speech c. reiteration   d. benefaction   e. ostentation

Circle the letter of the best ANTONYM for the word in bold-faced type.

8. widely **acclaimed**   a. execrated   b. expiated   c. ascribed d. known   e. subscribed
9. avoided **circumlocutions**   a. pseudonyms   b. homonyms c. straightforward statements   d. clamorous statements e. maledictions
10. deliver a(n) **declamation**   a. long speech   b. argument   c. forensic presentation   d. denial   e. quiet talk

EXERCISE 8B

Circle the letter of the sentence in which the word in bold-faced type is used incorrectly.

1. a. Even a **verbatim** account of the argument fails to convey its relevance.
  b. I paid back every penny **verbatim**.
  c. This plagiarized essay quotes the encyclopedia **verbatim**.
  d. You must repeat the oath **verbatim**.
2. a. Taxi drivers are **proverbial** dispersers of political opinion.
  b. "Let sleeping dogs lie" is **proverbial** wisdom.
  c. Roxelana, the consort of the Turkish sultan Suleiman the Magnificent, was the **proverbial** power behind the throne, controlling all appointments and decisions from the confines of the harem.
  d. A **proverbial** child uses gestures and expressions to communicate.
3. a. A good listener is rarely **loquacious**.
  b. Elizabeth Bennet was often embarrassed by her mother's **loquacity**, especially concerning her five daughters and their suitors.

    c. Even the **loquacious** detective Father Brown was struck dumb by the revelations.

    d. Use more **loquacious** words when you speak to your grandparents.

4. a. Before each debate our **forensics** coach has us prepare arguments both for and against the issue.

    b. The police prepared a **forensic** report for the trial that showed what kind of bullet had been fired and at what range and angle.

    c. Since the attention span of most Americans is no longer than the period between television commercials, **forensics** must now stress the quick, emotional appeal rather than the well-developed argument.

    d. At the **forensic**, teams from many different schools competed in different forms of public speaking.

5. a. The **acclaimed** writer Marguerite Yourcenar in 1980 became the first woman to be elected to the French Academy.

    b. One of the best-selling female recording artists of all time, Aretha Franklin, "Lady Soul," has received international **acclaim**.

    c. President Richard Nixon resigned rather than face Congressional **acclamations** about his role in the Watergate scandal.

    d. Lady Murasaki is universally **acclaimed** for her eleventh-century novel *The Tale of Genji*, about life and romance in Japanese courtly society.

6. a. Many of Jack London's novels show how the **clamor** of gold drew people to the rough Yukon country.

    b. Public **clamor** following the 1911 fire in the Triangle Shirt-waist Company that killed at least 141 people led to legislation of safe working conditions.

    c. Despite **clamorous** supporters of segregation, in 1961 Charlene Hunter Gault became the first African-American woman to matriculate at the University of Georgia.

    d. As soon as the Red Sox won the league pennant, fans **clamored** outside Fenway Park for World Series tickets.

7. a. **Linguists** have found that although the languages of Hungary and Finland are somewhat similar, they are unrelated to any other European language.

    b. One needs superior **linguist** skills to transcribe conversations from a tape recording.

    c. Many skilled **linguists** work for the U.N. General Assembly as simultaneous translators.

    d. Jakob Grimm, a nineteenth-century **linguist**, formulated Grimm's Law, which describes how Indo-European consonants shift in Germanic languages.

EXERCISE 8C Fill in each blank with the most appropriate word from Lesson 8. Use a word or any of its forms only once.

1. A Victorian child's education consisted of memorizing textbooks

   _____.

2. Swahili, a Bantu language of east and central Africa, is used

   throughout Africa as a _____ by peoples
   who speak many different languages and dialects.

3. At the university's _____ on medical ethics,
   several scientists spoke against genetic alteration as a way of
   producing "better people."

4. "Her employment was involuntarily terminated" is a

   _____ for "She didn't quit; she was fired."

5. "Kicking back" or "hanging loose" are informal _____
   for "relaxing."

6. The utilities company is sponsoring a _____
   on how to conserve energy in the workplace.

7. Because the government uses so many acronyms, new employees
   need a few weeks before they fully understand the bureaucratic

   _____.

8. The word *verbose* refers mainly to wordiness in writing; the word

   _____ refers mainly to wordiness in speech.

9. Historical _____ study the way in which
   languages evolve, a transformation that has made the Middle
   English of Geoffrey Chaucer only partially understandable to a
   speaker of modern English.

10. Most nineteenth-century politicians had great forensic stamina,

    ready to _____ for more than an hour at a
    time.

11. To sharpen their _____ skill, debaters must
    learn to improvise a speech on any topic.

12. Despite the _____ raised when the speed
    limit was reduced to 55 miles per hour, the public has come to
    recognize that many lives have been saved as a result.

13. Victorian novelists were often _____ because
    they were paid by the page.

EXERCISE 8D   Each word in italics can have more than one meaning. Write the meaning of the word implied by the context of the paragraph.

The skills required of politicians are very different from those needed by career diplomats. Where politicians need only to have (1) *forensic* ability in their own language, diplomats must be (2) *linguists*, able not just to speak but also to formulate tactful (3) *circumlocutions* in several languages. Whereas politicians seek a public (4) *forum*, hoping to win (5) *acclaim* and inspire (6) *clamorous* popularity, diplomats seek anonymity, effecting change behind the scenes. The career of the one illustrates the (7) *proverbial* "dog-eat-dog" political arena where every election may be the last; the career of the other exemplifies the (8) *proverbial* advice "Discretion is the better part of valor."

1. _____   5. _____

2. _____   6. _____

3. _____   7. _____

4. _____   8. _____

REVIEW EXERCISES FOR LESSONS 7 AND 8

1   Circle the letter of the best answer.

1. *glossa* : *lingua* : :
  a. indite : indict
  b. verbose : loquacious
  c. lingo : lingua franca
  d. tongue : tongue
  e. malediction : benediction
2. Which word is *not* derived from the root given?
  a. loquacious < *logos*
  b. proverbial < *verbum*
  c. affable < *fari*
  d. colloquium < *loqui*
  e. forensic < *forum*
3. Which word is *not* derived from *dicere*?
  a. circumlocution b. edict c. ditty d. benediction e. dictionary
4. Which word is *not* derived from *verbum*?
  a. proverbial b. verbatim c. verbose d. valediction e. verbal

2 Lessons 7 and 8 are about words. Add the word or phrase that completes the definitions.

    1. valedictory   words of _____

    2. verbatim   word _____

    3. verbose   using _____ words

    4. benediction words of _____

    5. indite   to _____ words

    6. interdiction words of _____

    7. acclamation words of _____

    8. diction   _____ of words

    9. dicta   words of _____

  10. malediction words of _____

3 Writing or Discussion Activities

1. Animal fables, like those of the Greek writer Aesop, and parables like those found in the Bible, often use analogy. They teach a lesson by illustrating it with a story. Make up a story that teaches a lesson by using an illustrative analogous situation. Your lesson might be something light, such as advice to new high school students, or practical, such as how to know when someone is joking, or more serious, such as a story illustrating a moral principle.

2. Indite a eulogy for yourself, someone you admire, or a fictional or historical character. Let your diction and tone be fitting to a serious and formal occasion.

3. During the Chinese Cultural Revolution, members of the Red Guard carried and quoted from little red books titled *The Sayings of Chairman Mao*, which contained many dicta and edicts of the former Chinese leader. Make up a short collection of such pronouncements typical of a person with whom you are familiar. You might choose a teacher, family member, friend, or personality from history or fiction. Entitle your parody *The Sayings of* ____.

4. People often use circumlocutions to avoid making embarrassing, insulting, or frank statements too directly. Write some circumlocutions to soften the frankness of these statements:

  a. If we don't eat soon, I'm going to faint.

  b. You looked better before you cut your hair.

  c. Your try-out was so bad you didn't even get the part of the messenger.

  d. This place is too expensive for me.

  e. I want to drop this class because it's boring.

PART TWO

Components
of the Universe

Earth and Air

Directions
1. Each KEY word is listed under a Greek or Latin root. Try to determine how the KEY word and the Familiar Words listed in the margin relate to the meaning of the root.
2. Using the diacritical marks, determine the pronunciation of each KEY word and say it aloud. Refer to the chart on the inside front cover of the book if you need help interpreting the diacritical marks.
3. Learn the definition(s) of each KEY word. Observe how the word is used in the sample sentence(s). Notice that some words have both a concrete and a metaphorical use.
4. Notice whether the KEY word is used as another part of speech or if it has an antonym.
5. Add to your understanding of the KEY words by observing all the additional information given in a lesson: the Latin epigraphs, the Challenge Words, and the Nota Bene references.
6. Practice using the words by completing the exercises.

LESSON 9

Terra firma.
Solid ground.

Key Words		
apogee	mountebank	repast
exhume	paramount	rustic
geocentric	pastoral	rusticate
humus	perigee	terra cotta
inter	promontory	terrestrial

Familiar Words
geography
geology
geometry
geophysics
geopolitics
George

Challenge Words
epigeal
Gaea
geode
geodesic dome
geomancy
geomorphic
geophagy
georgics
hyogeal
neogaea
notogaia

GAIA <G. "the earth"

1. apogee (ăp´ ə jē) [apo <G. "away from"]
n. 1. The point in its orbit when a planet or a satellite (usually the moon) is farthest from the earth.

At its **apogee** the moon's gravitational pull upon both water and land is weakest.

2. The highest point; culmination; apex.

Just as Margaret Mitchell's career as a novelist reached its **apogee** with the publication of *Gone with the Wind*, she died in an automobile accident.

Antonym: **perigee**

2. geocentric (jē´ ō sĕn´ trĭk)
[*centric = kentrikos < kentron* <G. "center"]
adj. 1. Referring to the center of the earth in measurement or observation.

When **geocentric** heat ruptures the earth's surface, volcanoes may spew forth lava, explode with fire, or belch boulders, cinders, and ash.

2. Considering the earth as the center of a planetary system.

As early as the third century B.C. Aristarchus of Samos countered **geocentric** assumptions with a detailed analysis of the earth's orbit around the sun.

NOTA BENE: Although *geocentricism* exists as a word referring to the now obsolete theory of the earth's central position in the universe, it does not appear at all in some dictionaries. The noun *heliocentrism* and adjective *heliocentric* [*helios* <G. "sun"], however, are legitimate words in both scientific and metaphorical usage.

3. perigee (pĕr´ ə jē) [*peri* <G. "around"]
n. The point in its orbit when a planet or a satellite (usually the moon) is nearest the earth.

A difference of 30,000 miles exists between the moon's **perigee** and apogee because of its elliptical orbit.

Antonym: **apogee**

TERRA <L. "earth," "land," "ground"

4. inter (ĭn tûr´) [*in* <L. "in"]
tr. v. To bury; to place in a grave.

"The evil that men do lives after them, / The good is oft **interred** with their bones," says Mark Antony in his eulogy for Julius Caesar.

internment, *n.*; **interred**, *adj.*
Antonym: **disinter**

5. terra cotta   (tĕr´ ə kŏt´ ə)
[*cotta* <Italian "cooked"]
n. Ceramic clay used in pottery, statuary, and construction. (Also used as an adjective.)

Terra cotta has long been a useful material for artisans and builders because it is inexpensive, durable, and versatile.

adj. Referring to the color of the clay, a reddish brown that may vary from gray or orange to dark brown.

Many buildings at the University of Virginia combine **terra cotta** brick with columns and doors painted white.

6. terrestrial   (tə rĕs´ trē əl)
adj. 1. Pertaining to the earth and its inhabitants.

On a bleak winter day the speaker in the poem "The Darkling Thrush" marvels at the bird's joyful song because "So little cause for carolings . . . / Was written on **terrestrial** things."

2. Referring to land as distinct from water or air.

Penguins are both **terrestrial** and aquatic animals, able to travel long distances both on land and in water.

terrestrial, *n.*
Antonyms: **celestial**; **aquatic**

HUMUS <L. "earth"

7. exhume   (ĕg zyo͞om´, ĭg zyo͞om´, ĕks hyo͞om´)
[*ex* <L. "from," "out of"]
tr. v. 1. To dig out of the ground or from a grave; to disinter.

In 1219 the University of Bologna became the first medieval institution to **exhume** bodies in order to train medical students in dissection.

2. To bring to light; to uncover.

From an attic trunk the granddaughter of a friend of Mark Twain **exhumed** a handwritten half of *The Adventures of Huckleberry Finn*, an exciting find for Twain scholars.

exhumation, *n.*; **exhumed**, *adj.*
Antonyms: **inhume**; **inter**

8. **humus** (hyōō´ məs)
n. Rich, dark organic material formed by decay of vegetable matter, essential to soil's fertility.

A noted British gardener, Victoria Sackville-West, recommends grass clippings to supply **humus**, thwart weeds, and maintain moisture in the soil.

MONS, MONTIS <L. "mountain"

9. **mountebank** (moun´ tə băngk´) [*bank = banco* <Italian *monte in banco*, "mount on a bench"; *montare* <L. "to climb a mountain"]
n. A swindler; a charlatan; a trickster.

P. T. Barnum is said to have changed the circus from a collection of **mountebanks** to a group of creditable performers in "The Greatest Show on Earth."

10. **paramount** (păr´ ə mount) [*para* <G. "beyond"]
adj. Of chief importance; primary; foremost.

For women trained as nurses early in the twentieth century a **paramount** concern became salaries and respect commensurate with their responsibilities.

11. **promontory** (prŏm´ ən tôr´ ē)
[*pro* <L. "before," "for"]
n. A high ridge of land jutting into a body of water; a headland.

Aegeus hurls himself from a **promontory** in despair when his son Theseus forgets to raise the white sail signaling his safe return from Crete after killing the Minotaur.

PASCO, PASCERE, PAVI, PASTUM <L. "to feed" (esp. cattle); "to nourish"
PASTOR <L. "shepherd"

12. pastoral (păs´ tə rəl, pä´ stər əl)
adj. 1. Pertaining to a Christian minister or the duties accompanying the office.

Pastoral attitudes of the clergymen in Anthony Trollope's Barsetshire novels range from sincere devotion to blatant self-interest.

2. Referring to life in open country or to fields for farming or grazing.

In the vast Australian bush, sheep, cattle, and horses graze on thousands of acres of **pastoral** land.

3. Pertaining to an idealized rural life.

Queen Marie Antoinette ordered construction of a **pastoral** retreat with costly "natural" gardens and an elaborate version of a working farm so that she could play at being a shepherdess.

pastoral, *n.*

13. repast (rĭ păst´) [*re* <L. "back," "again"]
n. A meal; food served at a meal.

In China, Egypt, India, and Indonesia a typical **repast** includes some form of maize, a plant native to America and introduced to other parts of the world after the arrival of Columbus.

RUS, RURIS <L. "open land," "country"

Familiar Word
rural

14. rustic (rŭs´ tĭk)
adj. Typical of country life and people; simple; rough.

Settlers on the Midwest prairie often had to live in **rustic** sod huts until they could import timber to build houses.

n. A rural person.

With their country dialect and superstitious beliefs, the **rustics** in Thomas Hardy's novels reflect a way of life that ended with the Industrial Revolution.

rusticity, *n.*

15. rusticate (rŭs´ tĭ kāt´)

intr. v. To go to the country.

Many New Yorkers like to **rusticate** in the Adirondacks during the summer.

tr. v. To cause to become rustic.

During the Chinese Cultural Revolution, government officials **rusticated** intellectuals and other professional people, confiscating or destroying their property.

NOTA BENE: The word *bucolic* [*bu* = *bous* <G. "cow" and *kolos* "herd"] can sometimes be a synonym for *pastoral* or *rustic*; a farm setting in a play or a site for a picnic could be *bucolic* or *pastoral* or *rustic*.

EXERCISE 9A

Circle the letter of the best SYNONYM for the word(s) in bold-faced type.

1. to stand on a **promontory**   a. principle   b. plateau   c. valley
   d. mountebank   e. headland
2. **terrestrial** animals   a. land-dwelling   b. aquatic   c. carnivorous
   d. tree-dwelling   e. geocentric
3. **pastoral** pleasures   a. urban   b. poetic   c. rustic   d. ordinary
   e. nightmarish
4. a savory **repast**   a. dinner   b. reminiscence   c. tidbit
   d. beverage   e. dessert
5. **terra cotta** sculpture   a. sand   b. charcoal   c. humus   d. clay
   e. stone
6. **humus** from the compost pile   a. grass   b. enriched soil
   c. ashes   d. decay   e. odor

Circle the letter of the best ANTONYM for the word in bold-faced type.

7. at the satellite's **perigee**   a. height   b. promontory   c. apogee
   d. distance   e. gravitation
8. a(n) **rustic** retreat   a. crude   b. primitive   c. corrupt
   d. pastoral   e. elegant
9. the **paramount** achievement   a. movie studio's   b. most obvious
   c. supreme   d. least important   e. least advantageous
10. a well-known **mountebank**   a. scoundrel   b. illiterate
    c. trustworthy person   d. climber   e. bank guard
11. to **rusticate** the children   a. isolate   b. citify   c. countrify
    d. stimulate   e. enrich

EXERCISE 9B   Circle the letter of the sentence in which the word in bold-faced type is used incorrectly.

1. a. Alexander the Great allegedly wept in his tent because, having reached the **apogee** of his career while still in his thirties, there were no more lands left for him to conquer.
  b. The eighth-century Chinese poet Tu Fu is said to have lifted the poetry of the Tang period to its **apogee**.
  c. The **apogee** of the spear felt cold against my chest.
  d. At its **apogee** the moon is 252,711 miles away from the earth; at its perigee, 221,500 miles.

2. a. Returning to his home where the family had buried possessions before deportation to concentration camps, Elie Wiesel **exhumed** a precious, rusty watch but placed it back in the earth.
  b. Descendants and scholars who **exhumed** James Boswell's letters and journals 130 years after his death discovered a candid record of personal foibles and eighteenth-century London life.
  c. Paleontologists who have **exhumed** dinosaur fossils report that herds once migrated from polar regions along an interior waterway extending the length of North America.
  d. The canal **exhumed** an odor of garbage and debris.

3. a. Medieval philosophers considered **terrestrial** order to be a reflection of celestial order.
  b. A **terrestrial** native of Asteroid B-612, the Little Prince travels through space to six planets before arriving at the seventh, earth.
  c. **Terrestrial** mapping by satellites provides meteorological and geographical information of seemingly infinite detail and quantity.
  d. When Columbus on his third voyage realized he had discovered a continent, not just another island, he called it a "**Terrestrial** Paradise."

4. a. To give her dead brother Polynices a peaceful afterlife, Antigone **interred** his body, thereby defying the law of Thebes.
  b. The prisoner of war learned English while **interred** in an internment camp.
  c. The Romans **interred** hundreds of bodies in the catacombs— tiered subterranean vaults outside the city gates along the Appian Way.
  d. In Emily Brontë's novel *Wuthering Heights*, Heathcliff asks to be **interred** beside his beloved Catherine.

5. a. Transplanted from rural Kentucky to Detroit during World War II, Harriette Arnow's protagonist in *The Dollmaker* finds her **rustic** ways both a social handicap and a source of strength.
  b. **Rustic** implements on display in the museum at Old Sturbridge Village include spinning wheels, scythes, and wooden handplows.

   c. Despite modern improvements in steel production to make it resistant to damage from moisture, extended exposure to rain can cause **rusticity**.

   d. The Beverly Hillbillies keep elements of **rusticity** while living in posh suburbia.

6. a. The mourners carried Beowulf to the **promontory** where mariners could see his funeral fire as befitted the heroic king of the Geats.

   b. After skirting the **promontory** known as Sugarloaf Mountain, the ship sailed into the harbor of Rio de Janeiro.

   c. Some public speakers develop an increasingly **promontory** style as they declaim.

   d. Despite cannons on the **promontory**, the fleet sailed into San Francisco Bay without incident.

7. a. Both Copernicus and Galileo recognized the inaccuracy of **geocentricism**, and both faced hostility from the church for their views.

   b. Fascinated by the idea of **geocentric** exploration, Jules Verne wrote of entering the depths through a volcano in Iceland and emerging from another in Italy.

   c. Since my family is the center of my world, I can call myself a genuine **geocentric**.

   d. Acquiring **geocentric** data is difficult because no instruments can withstand the extreme heat at the earth's core.

8. a. City folk rusticating in the country like to take a daily **pastoral** to keep them fit.

   b. Alexandra Bergson of *O Pioneers!* thrives in her **pastoral** setting: she loves the land and is proud of improvements made on her farm.

   c. Beethoven's *Pastoral* Symphony takes the listener to the country, beside a brook, amid a gathering of rural folk, and into a drenching thunderstorm that soon passes, to everyone's joy.

   d. Although not officially a detective, Father Dowling combines solving crimes with his **pastoral** duties.

EXERCISE 9C

Fill in each blank with the most appropriate word from Lesson 9. Use a word or any of its forms only once.

1. Harry Houdini, himself a master magician, crusaded against

_____ whose seeming marvels of magic were actually fraudulent.

2. When Felisa Rincón de Gautier became mayor of San Juan in

1946, her _____ concern was improving the living conditions of the poor.

3. Isak Dinesen's story "Babette's Feast" describes the extraordinary

_____ prepared by a superb chef.

4. The _____ theory that the earth orbits the sun did not completely give way to heliocentrism until the sixteenth century.

5. Boccaccio's *Decameron* is a collection of tales by a group of people

who _____ in the country in order to escape the pestilence sweeping their city.

6. Whether the moon is in _____, closest to the

earth, or in _____, farthest from it, only one of its faces is visible to terrestrials.

7. Inside the potting shed, the rich smell of _____ filled the air.

8. Known as the Pillars of Hercules, two _____ overlooking the Strait of Gibraltar separate Europe and Africa.

9. In Xi'an, China, archaeologists since 1974 have _____

more than two thousand terra cotta figures _____ two thousand years ago to accompany an emperor into the afterlife.

10. Traditional designs of Pueblo pottery, which is made of

_____, record twenty-four centuries of history in the Southwest.

EXERCISE 9D   Each word in italics can have more than one meaning. Write the meaning of the word implied by the context of the paragraph.

The pantheism prevalent at the (1) *apogee* of the romantic period in England led to an intense interest in all things "natural." In contrast to the sophisticated elegance of eighteenth-century art, in which country life appeared only as a classical (2) *pastoral*, with shepherds frolicking among Greek ruins, nineteenth-century art focused on realistic (3) *rustics*. Whereas classical art abounded with Olympian gods clad in golden sandals, romantic art depicted distinctly (4) *terrestrial* beings wearing rough boots stained (5) *terra cotta* from convincingly real mud.

This interest in the natural went beyond the visual arts. Many who once gravitated to the capitals of Europe began to (6) *rusticate*, seeking out "wild" places like the Hebrides and the Swiss Alps where they could experience the grandeur of nature and uncontaminated country life. Once rejected as (7) *rustic*, folk crafts like wood carving and basketry now found a place in fashionable drawing rooms, and many forgotten collections of folk songs and folktales were (8) *exhumed* and published. This appreciation for natural landscape and folk art has outlived the romantic period and persists into the twentieth century.

1. _____   5. _____
2. _____   6. _____
3. _____   7. _____
4. _____   8. _____

LESSON 10

In aere picardi; in mare venaris.
To fish in the air; to hunt in the sea.*

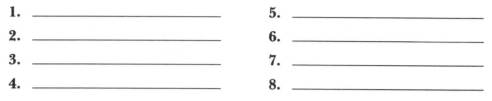

Key Words

animus	equanimity	hyperventilation
aspiration	ether	phantasm
diaphanous	ethereal	pusillanimous
dispirited	hyperbole	sycophant
epiphany	hyperborean	vent

Familiar Words
animal
animation
inanimate
magnanimity
unanimity

Challenge Word
longanimity

ANIMA <L. "wind," "air"
ANIMUS <L. "mind," "soul"

1. **animus** (ăn´ ə məs)
   n. 1. A powerful feeling of hostility or antagonism; hatred.

   In *Moby Dick*, relentless **animus** drives Captain Ahab to pursue that incarnation of evil, the white whale, to avenge the loss of a leg.

   2. An animating spirit.

   Anne Sullivan's tutelage provided the **animus** for Helen Keller's emergence from the dark silence that had been her life.

2. **equanimity** (ē´ kwə nĭm´ ə tē, ĕ´ kwə nĭm´ ə tē)
   [*aequus* <L. "equal"]
   n. Composure and calm in stressful conditions; equilibrium.

   Hospital trauma centers depend on the **equanimity** of their doctors and nurses as they cope with continual emergencies.

   equanimous, *adj.*

---

*Said of persons attempting things for which they are unsuited by nature or circumstances.

3. **pusillanimous** (pyŏŏ´ sə lăn´ ə məs)
[*pusillus* <L. "very little"]
adj. Cowardly; fearful.

The Cowardly Lion travels to the Land of
Oz, where he hopes the Wizard's powers will transform him forever
from **pusillanimous** to courageous.

pusillanimity, *n.*

AETHER <L. "upper air," "clear sky"
AITHER <G. "air"

4. **ether** (ē´ thər)
n. 1. The regions of space beyond the earth's atmosphere; the
heavens.

In 1957 the Russian satellite *Sputnik* launched the Space Age and the
incipient presence of earthlings into the **ether**.

2. A highly flammable liquid anesthetic.

Queen Victoria's acceptance of an anesthetic during childbirth sanctioned the use of chloroform and **ether** for other women.

etherize, *v.*

5. **ethereal** (ĭ thĭr´ ē əl)
adj. 1. Spiritlike in lightness and delicacy.

The celesta, a small keyboard instrument, produces such **ethereal** tones
that Tchaikovsky used it for the "Dance of the Sugar-Plum Fairy" in
The Nutcracker.

2. Heavenly; celestial.

In "To a Skylark" William Wordsworth
addresses the bird as "**Ethereal** ministrel!
pilgrim of the sky!"

etherealize, *v.*

PHAINEIN <G. "to show," "to appear"

Familiar Words
cellophane
emphasis
fantasy
phantom
phase
phenomena
phenomenon
Tiffany

6. **diaphanous** (dī ăf´ ə nəs)
[*dia* <G. "through"]
adj. Allowing light to show through;
translucent; delicate.

Isadora Duncan shocked the public with her
unconventional style of dancing and her
diaphanous Grecian drapery.

7. **epiphany**   (ĭ pĭf´ ə nē)   [*epi* <G. "on"]
   n. 1. A revelatory manifestation of a divine being.

   In the Bible, the presence of an angel with whom Jacob wrestles all night provides an **epiphany**: evidence of his favor with God.

   2. A revelation; a flash of understanding of the true nature of something.

   A middle-of-the-night **epiphany** inspired the abolitionist Julia Ward Howe to indite the words of "The Battle Hymn of the Republic," which became a Civil War anthem.

   3. (capitalized) A Christian festival, January 6, celebrating the visit of the Wise Men to the Christ Child.

   "Twelfth night," which occurs on the eve of **Epiphany**, marks the end of the twelve days of Christmas.

8. **phantasm**   (făn´ tăz əm)
   n. A phantom; an apparition; something unreal, as in a dream or a vision.

   Among the Sioux people, sacred vision quests produced **phantasms**, figures with instructive or healing powers, emanating from thunder, clouds, and other natural phenomena.

   phantasmic, *adj.*

9. **sycophant**   (sĭk´ ə fənt)
   [*syco* = *sukon* <G. "fig." Sycophants identified thieves and smugglers of figs to the police.]
   n. A flatterer seeking favors or gain; a servile self-seeker; a toady.

   Shakespeare's *Richard II* shows that the flattery of **sycophants** can blind a ruler to serious problems in the realm.

   sycophancy, *n.*; **sycophantic**, *adj.*

SPIRITUS <L. "breath"
SPIRO, SPIRARE, SPIRAVI, SPIRATUM <L. "to blow gently"

10. **aspiration**   (ăs´ pər ā´ shən)   [*a* = *ad* <L. "to," "toward"]
    n. 1. Strong desire for achievement; ambition toward a long-range goal.

    In 1972 Representative Shirley Chisholm's **aspiration** was to be the Democratic presidential candidate; however, she lost the nomination to George McGovern, who lost the election to Richard Nixon.

Challenge Words
con spiritu
inspirit
spiritualism
spiritus mundi
spiritus sanctus
suspire
transpire

2. Expulsion of breath in speaking.

To become a believable English lady, Eliza Doolittle must perfect the **aspiration** of *h* by making a candle flame flicker when she says, "Hertford, Hereford, and Hampshire."

aspirant, *n.*; **aspirate**, *v.*; **aspire**, *v.*

11. **dispirited**   (dĭs spĭr´ ə təd)
[*dis* <L. "apart"]
adj. Dejected; discouraged; gloomy.

Although repeatedly **dispirited** by failed experiments and insufficient funds, Canadian doctors Charles Best and Frederick Banting were able in 1921 to isolate insulin as a cure for diabetes.

dispirit, *v.*

HUPER <G. "over," "above"

Familiar Words
hyperbola
hypercritical
hypersensitive
hypertension

12. **hyperbole**   (hī pûr´ bə lē)
n. An exaggeration; a figure expressing excess.

"I solved my math problems like Einstein discovering the Theory of Relativity" is an example of **hyperbole**.

hyperbolic, *adj.*; **hyperbolism**, *n.*; **hyperbolize**, *v.*

Challenge Words
Hyperion
hyperkinesia
hypersonic
hyperthermia

13. **hyperborean**   (hī´ pər bô´ rē ən,
hī´ pər bô rē´ ăn)
[*boreios* <G. "northern"]
adj. 1. Far north; Arctic.

In Greek mythology members of an unnamed **hyperborean** people were known for their piety and worship of Apollo.

2. Very cold; frigid.

Without airtight space capsules, astronauts could not survive the **hyperborean** temperatures of the ether.

NOTA BENE: Consult a dictionary for forty more words containing the prefix *hyper*, most of them pertaining to mathematics or medical conditions.

VENTUS <L. "wind"

Familiar Words
ventilate
ventilator

14. **hyperventilation**   (hī´ pər vĕn tĭ lā´ shən)
[*hyper* = *huper* <G. "above," "beyond"]
n. The condition of taking abnormally fast, deep breaths.

Challenge Words
ventage
ventail

The sudden anxiety some scuba divers experience when they encounter sharks can cause **hyperventilation**.

NOTA BENE: You may have heard the verb *hyperventilate*; although it is often used, it is not considered standard usage and most dictionaries do not include it.

15. vent (vĕnt)

n. An outlet; an opening for passage of liquids, fumes, or sometimes air.

Trapped by an avalanche, the skiers frantically clawed a **vent** in the snow.

tr. v. To utter; to express, especially in relieving strong feelings.

Protesters for nuclear disarmament gathered at the courthouse to **vent** their anxieties about the fate of the world.

NOTA BENE: Before leaving the collection of words associated with *air*, consider the Latin verb meaning "to blow"—*flo, flare, flavi, flatum*—giving us these familiar English words: *inflate, deflate, flavor, flute,* and *soufflé.* Challenge words are *afflatus, conflation, flatus,* and *flatulence.*

EXERCISE 10A

Circle the letter of the best SYNONYM for the word in bold-faced type.

1. a(n) **ethereal** beauty   a. eerie   b. eternal   c. changeable
   d. delicate   e. rugged
2. to experience **hyperventilation**   a. loss of altitude   b. strong
   breezes   c. asphyxiation   d. very fast, deep breaths   e. loss of
   oxygen
3. **venting** their anger   a. combining   b. increasing   c. expressing
   d. suppressing   e. sharing
4. a(n) **diaphanous** cloak   a. heavy   b. elaborate   c. shiny
   d. invisible   e. filmy
5. sustained **animus**   a. discouragement   b. animation   c. hatred
   d. breathing   e. affection

Circle the letter of the best ANTONYM for the word in bold-faced type.

6. **equanimity** under siege   a. generosity   b. calmness   c. partiality
   d. panic   e. incivility
7. **pusillanimous** contestants   a. faint-hearted   b. courageous
   c. foul-smelling   d. animated   e. circumscribed
8. seeing a **phantasm**   a. ghost   b. material object   c. point of light
   d. miracle   e. shadow

9. **hyperborean** regions   a. legendary   b. frigid   c. tropical
   d. forested   e. unpopulated
10. **dispirited** after the loss   a. optimistic   b. pale   c. ethereal
    d. spiritual   e. downhearted
11. a notorious **sycophant**   a. invalid   b. cheat   c. flatterer
    d. malcontent   e. slanderer
12. a frequent user of **hyperboles**   a. games of chance
    b. understatements   c. exaggerations   d. tall stories   e. geometric
    figures

EXERCISE 10B   Circle the letter of the sentence in which the word in bold-faced type is used incorrectly.

1. a. Although Scott Joplin **aspired** to acclaim as a classical musician, his fame now rests on his ragtime compositions.
   b. Their daily **aspiration** was to complete their homework immediately after baseball practice.
   c. In cardiopulmonary resuscitation (CPR), pressure on the lung cavity stimulates **aspiration**.
   d. An **aspiring** astronaut, Mae C. Jemison became the first African-American woman in the training program of the National Aeronautics and Space Administration.
2. a. For many viewers, the **ethereal** drama of a total eclipse is the thrill of a lifetime.
   b. Anna Pavlova's frothy white tutu and fluttering gestures in Fokine's *The Dying Swan* made her look **ethereal**, as if she could rise into the air like a swan.
   c. **Ethereal** dosage of patients undergoing surgery made the relief of pain a significant breakthrough in the practice of medicine.
   d. Floating across the mountain lake at dusk, the echo of our shouts grew fainter and more **ethereal**.
3. a. Learning that his wife can still mourn the death of a youthful love becomes a painful **epiphany** after a dancing party in James Joyce's story, "The Dead."
   b. Because the Feast of **Epiphany** commemorates the ceremony of gifts to the infant Jesus, in many countries it is celebrated with gift-giving.
   c. Watching children send messages by tapping lengths of wood served Dr. René Laennec as an **epiphany** leading to his invention of the stethoscope.
   d. The harpist's arpeggios and **epiphanies** thrilled the audience.
4. a. Speeding through the **ether** on his winged sandals, the mythical god Mercury delivered messages.
   b. Although a more satisfactory pain-killer than alcohol or opium, **ether** has been superseded by nitrous oxide and cyclopropane.

    c. The three-hour balloon excursion into the **ether** gave the
travelers a look at their neighborhood.

    d. The veterinarian **etherized** the grizzly bear long enough to
examine it.

5. a. The infidelity of Jason, the Argonaut, stirs such **animus** in his
wife Medea that she slays their two children.

    b. In the novel *The Thief and the Dogs* the **animus** of the central
character toward a former friend fuels a single-minded program
of revenge.

    c. Listening to popular music while studying provides useful
background **animus** for concentration and hard work.

    d. The experience of poverty early in life can provide the **animus** to
escape.

6. a. In 1990 a camera on the space shuttle *Columbia* as it traveled in
space photographed a **diaphanous** cloud formation from an
explosion calculated to have taken place 20,000 years ago.

    b. Berthe Morisot's painting "The Cradle" depicts a mother gazing
at her sleeping baby within a crib curtained by **diaphanous** white
netting.

    c. Fluttering **diaphanous** wings, the dragonfly skimmed the surface
of the pond.

    d. The jeweler carefully placed an enormous **diaphanous** diamond
in the center of a black velvet cushion.

7. a. Because the cave had a natural **vent**, it was never smoky.

    b. The museum displayed a medieval gown with sleeve **vents** lined
in red silk.

    c. Some people are able to **vent** their frustrations through painting,
writing, or playing basketball.

    d. The children pranced about and **vented** merrily in the park.

EXERCISE 10C

Fill in each blank with the most appropriate word from Lesson 10. Use
a word or any of its forms only once.

    1. Although _____ after failing to win a medal
in the Olympic luge competition, the team vowed to try again.

    2. When _____ winds blow south from Canada
or Siberia, Chicagoans wrap up in their warmest clothing.

    3. The playwright R. B. Sheridan satirizes the ritual of dueling as Bob
Acres, a rustic, challenges a rival in love but grows

    _____ when faced with actually shooting him.

    4. In Toni Morrison's novel *Beloved*, Sethe's last daughter makes

    appearances as a _____ before becoming a
person in the flesh.

5. When Ben Jonson's character Volpone pretends to be on his

deathbed, he makes fools of hovering _____ hoping to flatter him into a legacy.

6. A very expensive item can stimulate _____:
in English, "It costs an arm and a leg; in Spanish, "It costs an eye from the face" (*Cuesta un ojo de la cara*).

7. The insistent heckling of protesters at the back of the hall upset the speaker, who was suddenly overcome by an attack of

_____.

8. The word *herb* offers a lesson in pronunciation: the British

_____ the *h* while Americans treat it as a silent letter.

9. In *Star Trek: The Second Generation* the unflappable Guinan, played

by Whoopi Goldberg, keeps her _____ no matter what perils her crew faces.

10. Conflict in the _____ grows tense in Isaac Asimov's novel *Foundation* in a battle over control of a galaxy.

11. Joan of Arc experienced a(n) _____ when in a vision she saw herself summoned to lead French troops to victory over the English invaders.

EXERCISE 10D   In the story below, replace the word or phrase in italics with a key word (or any of its forms) from Lesson 10.

In dreams amazing things can happen. Take the dream of Celeste Azul, for example. Enjoying a bit of TV with her dog Perrito before bedtime, she saw a 1963 picture of the first woman in space, Soviet cosmonaut Valentina Tereshkova-Nikolayeva, traveling in the (1) *regions of space beyond the earth's atmosphere.*

No sooner had Celeste fallen asleep than she was mysteriously catapulted into a(n) (2) *intensely frigid* world, colder than Earth's arctic regions. Encased in a space suit, she was floating outside her satellite. Her first reaction was (3) *deeply gasping for air*, but she quickly recovered as she looked out at her terrestrial home. That "blue ball," as Valentina had described it, seemed a(n) (4) *ghostly illusion*, and Celeste became a(n) (5) *light and airy* native of the universe, enjoying blissful (6) *composure and calm* as if she were not moving at many miles a second.

When Perrito's barking woke her up, Celeste's dream had materialized into a(n) (7) *long-range goal* to be an astronaut. Her space visit was a(n) (8) *moment of revelation* providing the (9) *animating spirit, or driving force* for classes in math and science, essential for reaching her goal.

1. _____   6. _____
2. _____   7. _____
3. _____   8. _____
4. _____   9. _____
5. _____

REVIEW EXERCISES FOR LESSONS 9 AND 10

1. Which Latin word means the same as the Greek word *gaia*?
a. *humus* b. *pastor* c. *rus* d. *terra* e. *ventus*

2. Which word is *not* derived from the Latin word *anima*?
a. animal b. unanimity c. ethereal d. pusillanimous
e. animation

3. Which word is *not* derived from the Greek word *phainein*?
a. phantasm b. diaphanous c. equanimity d. epiphany
e. sycophant

4. Which set of three roots is most directly associated with "air"?
a. *rus, huper, ventus*
b. *spirare, aether, terra*
c. *huper, anima, aether*
d. *phainein, mons, spirare*
e. *aether, spirare, ventus*

5. Which pair contains no common Latin or Greek root?
a. hyperbole—hyperventilate
b. promontory—mountebank
c. animus—diaphanous
d. dispirited—aspiration
e. pastoral—repast

6. mountebank : fraudulent : :
a. phantasm : real
b. rustic : polished
c. pastor : selfish
d. aspirant : hopeful
e. sycophant : self-sacrificing

7. terrestrial : earth : :
a. exhumed : mountains
b. ethereal : sky
c. inanimate : water
d. hyperbolic : air
e. diaphanous : humus

8. animus : hating : :
   a. hyperbole : excited
   b. perigee : paramount
   c. epiphany : sad
   d. hyperventilation : exhausted
   e. equanimity : calm

2 Matching: On the line at the left, write the letter of the phrase that is best described by the adjective.

_____ **1.** vented	A. grazing sheep, cows, and goats
_____ **2.** hyperborean	B. a person afraid of his or her own shadow
_____ **3.** diaphanous	C. a person speaking of millions of daily tasks
_____ **4.** terrestrial	D. a chimney
_____ **5.** ethereal	E. minerals at the center of the earth
_____ **6.** pusillanimous	F. an arctic wind
_____ **7.** phantasmic	G. a ghostly figure in the shadows
_____ **8.** hyperbolic	H. burrowing snakes and foxes
_____ **9.** pastoral	I. a twinkling star
_____ **10.** geocentric	J. a gauze curtain

3 Writing or Discussion Activities

1. Sometimes you experience an *epiphany*, a flash of understanding about yourself, someone you know, a character in a book, or an idea. Have you recognized such a moment in your life or in the literature that you have been reading? Describe such a moment, briefly explaining the situation, the character to whom it happens (if other than yourself), and the significance of the revelation for you or that character.

2. What are your *aspirations*? Choose one and describe the goal that you aspire to—a position in a school organization, a job, attendance at a school or college, or whatever your aspiration.

3. Do you indulge in *hyperbole*? Hear yourself talking, listen to your friends, notice hyperboles in books you are reading, and become a collector of these exaggerations. Try inventing some of your own, expressing feelings of embarrassment, hunger, panic, disgust, affection, or any strong emotion.

Fire and Water

Parva saepe scintilla contempta excitavit incendium.
Often a small ignored spark has started a fire.
—Q. CURTIUS RUFUS

	Key Words	
caustic	flagrant	pyre
cauterize	flamboyant	pyromania
conflagration	incendiary	pyrotechnics
effervescent	incense	scintilla
fervid	inflammatory	scintillate

FERVO, FERVERE, FERVI <L. "to be boiling hot"

1. **fervid** (fûr´ vĭd)
   adj. Full of intense passion or zeal.

   The governor's campaign oratory inspired **fervid** support.

   fervency, *n.*; **fervent**, *adj.*; **fervor**, *n.*

2. **effervescent** (ĕf´ ər vĕs´ ənt) [*e* = *ex* <L. "away from," "out of"]
   adj. 1. Bubbling up from a liquid.

Carbonated liquids are naturally **effervescent**, but effervescence becomes more powerful at higher altitudes, as hikers often discover.

2. Very excited; bubbling over with high spirits.

Effervescent throngs cheered in 1989 when they saw the Berlin Wall begin to crumble after separating East and West Germany for twenty-eight years.

effervesce, *v.*; **effervescence**, *n.*

FLAGRO, FLAGRARE, FLAGRAVI, FLAGRATUM <L. "to glow," "to burn," "to blaze"

3. **conflagration**   (kŏn´ flə grā´ shən)
[*con* = *cum* <L. "with"]
n. A large and destructive fire.

Despite the 1988 **conflagration** that blackened thousands of acres in Yellowstone National Park, abundant green shoots appeared the following spring.

conflagrant, *adj.*

4. **flagrant**   (flā´ grənt)
adj. Shockingly evident; outrageously conspicuous.

Amnesty International is an organization that protests **flagrant** violations of human rights around the world.

flagrance, *n.*; **flagrancy**, *n.*

FLAMMA <L. "flame"

Familiar Words
flame
flamingo
flammable
inflammable

Challenge Word
flambeau

5. **inflammatory**   (ĭn flăm´ ə tô´ rē)   [*in* = "in"]
adj. 1. Arousing strong emotion, especially anger or hostility.

Alice Hamilton's investigation of toxic substances in the workplace made her an **inflammatory** presence to factory owners, but her efforts accelerated action to set federal safety standards for working conditions.

2. Pertaining to redness, swelling, or pain following an infection or injury.

Mosquito bites cause itching, but bee stings inject an **inflammatory**—sometimes even deadly—substance.

inflame, *v.*; **inflammation**, *n.*

6. **flamboyant** (flăm boi´ ənt)
adj. Colored or decorated in a showy way; having a showy appearance or manner.

Flamboyant revelers at Carnaval in Rio de Janeiro have a last fling before the austerity of Lent, the forty days ending on Easter.

flamboyance, *n.*

NOTA BENE: *Flammable* and *inflammable* have the same meaning: "easily ignited." *Inflammable* can also mean "easily angered."

INCENDO, INCENDERE, INCENDI, INCENSUM <L. "to set on fire"

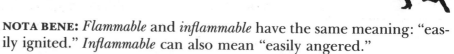

7. **incendiary** (ĭn sĕn´ dē ĕr´ ē)
adj. 1. Designed or intended to cause a fire.

Kurt Vonnegut's satirical novel *Slaughterhouse Five* attacks the **incendiary** bombing of Dresden by Allied forces that killed thousands and decimated a city known for its art and architectural treasures.

2. Tending to stir up strife; inflammatory.

Often **incendiary** in her fight against apartheid in South Africa, Helen Suzman has become a champion for both whites and blacks.

n. A person who maliciously burns his or her own or another's property for monetary advantage.

After a series of fires traceable to **incendiaries** in seventeenth-century Boston, city leaders not only sought the offenders, but also improved fire-fighting equipment.

incendiarism, *n.*

8. **incense** (ĭn sĕns´)
tr. v. To infuriate; to enrage.

In the mock-epic poem "The Rape of the Lock," an admirer **incenses** Belinda when he forcibly snips off a lock of her hair.

NOTA BENE: Remember the difference in pronunciation between the verb *incense* (ĭn sĕns´) and the noun *incense* (ĭn´ sĕns), meaning "an aromatic substance having a pleasant smell."

<table>
<tr><td>

Familiar Words
caliber
calm
holocaust

</td></tr>
</table>

<table>
<tr><td>

Challenge Word
encaustic

</td></tr>
</table>

KAIEIN <G. "to burn"

9. caustic   (kôs´ tĭk)
adj. 1. Able to burn or eat away by chemical action.

Because battery fluid, like other alkaline substances, is **caustic**, used batteries must be disposed of in special toxic dump sites.

2. Sarcastic; marked by a biting wit.

When an American president complained that Alice Roosevelt Longworth's large hat made it difficult for him to give her a kiss, her **caustic** reply was, "That's why I wear it."

10. cauterize   (kô´ tə rīz)
tr. v. To burn with a hot iron or a chemical to destroy abnormal tissue and/or to stop infection and/or bleeding.

When a rural doctor was not available, the local blacksmith could use his tools to **cauterize** a cut or puncture, sometimes preventing infection in the wound.

cauterization, *n.*; **cautery**, *n.*

<table>
<tr><td>

Challenge Words
empyrean
pyroclastic
pyrogenic
pyromancy
pyrometer
pyrosis

</td></tr>
</table>

PUR <G. "fire"

11. pyre   (pīr)
n. A pile of wood, etc., for burning a corpse as part of a funeral rite; any pile of combustible materials.

The phoenix, a mythic bird, periodically burns itself on a **pyre** but flies up from it reborn.

12. pyrotechnics   (pī´ rə tĕk´ nĭks, pîr´ ə tĕk´ nĭks)
[*technē* <G. "a working with hands," "a craft"]
n. 1. A display of fireworks

The United States celebrated its bicentennial with **pyrotechnics** in the sky above the Statue of Liberty.

2. A spectacular display of virtuosity in music, writing, wit, or other accomplishment.

A one-man orchestra, Bobby McFerrin produces musical **pyrotechnics** with a singing range of four octaves and rhythmic sounds from his body surfaces.

pyrotechnic, *adj.*; **pyrotechnical**, *adj.*

13. **pyromania** (pī´ rō mā´ nē ə, pī´ rō mān´ yə)
[*mania* <G. "excessive desire for (something)"]
n. A compulsion to set things on fire.

A person afflicted with **pyromania** may be uncontrollably driven to start a fire, but may rush to help fire fighters extinguish it.

pyromaniac, *n.*

SCINTILLA <L. "spark"

14. **scintilla** (sĭn tĭl´ ə)
n. A very small amount; a bit; an iota.

Jurors are instructed to vote "not guilty" if they have even a **scintilla** of doubt in their minds about the defendant's guilt.

15. **scintillate** (sĭn´ tə lāt)
intr. v. 1. To give off sparks; to flash; to sparkle.

The queen's jewels **scintillated** in the soft light.

2. To be animated or brilliant.

In film and on stage, Mary Martin **scintillated**, notably as Nellie Forbush in the musical *South Pacific* and as Peter Pan.

scintillating, *adj.*; **scintillation**, *n.*

NOTA BENE: The Latin word *sol*, meaning "sun," belongs in this lesson of "hot" words. Some derivatives are *solar*; *parasol*; *solarium*, "a sun room"; and *solstice*, June 22 and December 22, the two times in the year when the sun is at the most southern or northern point of its eliptic. The next time you visit a drugstore notice the number of products using some form of *sol* in their names.

EXERCISE 11A   Circle the letter of the best SYNONYM for the word in bold-faced type.

1. a sacrificial **pyre**   a. hoard   b. attack   c. rite   d. combustible pile   e. funeral
2. a(n) **caustic** remark   a. rationalizing   b. scintillating   c. soothing d. sarcastic   e. fervid
3. **inflammatory** headlines   a. bright red   b. placating c. incendiary   d. false   e. informative
4. **flamboyant** uniforms   a. floatable   b. protective   c. eclectic d. rustic   e. ostentatious
5. **scintillating** conversation   a. inflammatory   b. tedious c. incendiary   d. sarcastic   e. brilliant
6. to **cauterize** a wound   a. burn   b. inflict   c. heal   d. cut e. bleed

Circle the letter of the best ANTONYM for the word in bold-faced type.

7. a hired **incendiary** a. firebrand   b. arsonist   c. agnostic
  d. fire fighter   e. pyromaniac
8. naturally **effervescent** spring water   a. bubbling   b. toxic
  c. fervid   d. tasteless   e. sluggish
9. **incensed** by injustice   a. harmed   b. calmed   c. pursued
  d. enraged   e. challenged
10. named in **flagrant** graffiti   a. obliterated   b. verbose
  c. hyperbolic   d. inflammatory   e. eclectic
11. **fervid** connoisseurs   a. theocratic   b. dispirited   c. hyperborean
  d. epigrammatic   e. incendiary
12. treatment for a **pyromaniac**   a. schizophrenic   b. fire-setter
  c. forest ranger   d. fire-hater   e. burn victim

EXERCISE 11B   Circle the letter of the sentence in which the word in bold-faced type is
used incorrectly.

1. a. Bruises, **inflammations**, and sprains are inevitable for players of
    contact sports like football.
  b. Known as "La Pasionaria," Dolores Ibarruri became an
    inflammatory figure during the Spanish Civil War for her
    Loyalist support, for which she was ejected from Spain.
  c. The accusation of plagiarism set up an **inflammatory** exchange at
    the meeting of scholars.
  d. A government office has declared that children's clothing should
    be made of safe, **inflammatory** materials.
2. a. The public health workers were **incensed** by the number of
    people who refused immunization against polio.
  b. The smoke from the pine logs **incensed** the whole house.
  c. The refusal of the Daughters of the American Revolution to let
    Marian Anderson sing in Constitution Hall in Washington so
    incensed Eleanor Roosevelt that she resigned from that
    organization.
  d. The teasing and tricks of Bugs Bunny unceasingly **incense** Elmer
    Fudd.
3. a. Said to have begun when Mrs. O'Leary's cow kicked over a
    lantern, the 1871 **conflagration** in Chicago killed hundreds of
    people and did $200 million worth of damage.
  b. Samuel Pepys' famous *Diary* describes the four-day **conflagration**
    in 1666 that destroyed 13,000 houses in London.
  c. National political conventions feature **conflagrations** of banners,
    placards, and pennants naming a favored candidate.
  d. Water bucket brigades could not control the **conflagrations** that
    devoured wooden houses of early Jamestown and Plymouth.

4. a. Beware of her **caustic** sense of humor!
  b. When required to clean an expensive rug he has deliberately muddied, the vengeful incendiary in William Faulkner's story "Barn Burning" uses **caustic** lye and returns the rug ruined.
  c. When you cut yourself shaving, use a **caustic** to stop the bleeding.
  d. Samuel Johnson was being **caustic** when he said, "That fellow seems to me to possess but one idea, and that is a wrong one."

5. a. Hardly a **scintilla** of documentation exists to ascertain the intensity of love existing between Ann Rutledge and Abraham Lincoln.
  b. The black velvet gown reflected light from hundreds of tiny **scintillas**.
  c. Don't alter a **scintilla** of that wonderful essay.
  d. Even a **scintilla** of a foreign chemical in the blood can disqualify an athlete.

6. a. Blame for the 1934 disastrous fire aboard the luxury ship *Morro Castle* fell on an **incendiary**, a disgruntled crew member, along with the captain's inadequate fire precautions.
  b. A skillful negotiator must know how to cool **incendiary** tempers during mediation.
  c. As an **incendiary** to efficiency, we get a half day off whenever we surpass our quota.
  d. The Inferno in Dante's *The Divine Comedy* includes a group of vengefully irascible souls who must suffer the perpetual punishment of **incendiary** rain.

7. a. The writer Tom Wolfe prepares you for his **pyrotechnics** with the title *The Kandy-Kolored Tangerine-Flake Streamline Baby*.
  b. When Kathleen Battle sings Mozart, the **pyrotechnics** flash.
  c. Some towns have built rinks where expert skateboarders can show off their **pyrotechnics**.
  d. A playful **pyrotechnic** lit the pyre in the stadium too soon and spoiled the homecoming ceremonies.

EXERCISE 11C

Circle the letter of the most appropriate pair of words to complete the following sentences.

1. To the music of Tchaikovsky the trapeze artists _____ in their sequined tights and drew rapturous applause for their _____ and daring.
  a. effervesced . . . pyromania
  b. scintillated . . . pyrotechnics
  c. inflamed . . . fervor
  d. incensed . . . scintillation
  e. cauterized . . . flamboyance

2. Fire fighters make a distinction between motivations of people who set fires deliberately: _____, which is an uncontrollable urge, and arson, or _____, which is an act of revenge motivated by self-interest, such as setting one's own property on fire to collect the insurance.
   a. inflammation . . . conflagration
   b. cautery . . . pyrotechnics
   c. pyromania . . . incendiarism
   d. fervor . . . scintillation
   e. flagrance . . . flamboyance

3. After the 1906 San Francisco earthquake had broken water, gas, and electric lines, the worst damage followed: a(n) _____, which both fire fighters and citizens fought with _____.
   a. pyre . . . incense
   b. incendiary . . . flagrance
   c. inflammation . . . pyrotechnics
   d. scintillation . . . flamboyance
   e. conflagration . . . fervor

4. Although Dorothy Parker's conversation sparkled with witty epigrams, she was _____ toward a fellow writer: "The only 'ism' she believes in is 'plagiarism.' "
   a. effervescently inflammatory
   b. pyrotechnically fervid
   c. flamboyantly incensed
   d. flagrantly caustic
   e. fervidly pyromaniacal

5. In the sixteenth century Spanish gentlemen were elegant, even _____, in black suits adorned with ribbons and feathers, and _____ with gold and silver thread and precious stones.
   a. pyrotechnic . . . effervescent
   b. flamboyant . . . scintillating
   c. flagrant . . . fervid
   d. incensed . . . flagrant
   e. caustic . . . inflammable

6. Having no _____ of tolerance for the practice of *suttee*, the Hindu custom requiring a nobleman's widow to burn herself on her husband's _____, the British governors in India proscribed it.
   a. scintilla . . . pyre
   b. fervor . . . conflagration
   c. effervescence . . . pyromania
   d. flagrance . . . pyrotechnics
   e. inflammation . . . cautery

EXERCISE 11D   Replace the word or phrase in italics with a key word (or any of its forms) from Lesson 11.

History is replete with records of accidental fires as well as (1) *notoriously conspicuous* acts of warfare with fire as a weapon. Some fiery accidents have been instructive, as was the case with the German dirigible *Hindenburg* in 1936. After a successful transatlantic flight, the airship prepared to land at Lakehurst, New Jersey. The welcoming throng on the ground below may hardly have seen a (2) *very small bit* of flame begin to nibble at the silver surface before it suddenly burst into a fireball that slowly writhed and withered on its way to the ground. Although the reason for the fatal spark remains unclear, some people claim that a(n) (3) *person deliberately setting a fire* had hidden a bomb inside the vast interior of the airship for political reasons.

Of fires to help win a war, the destruction of Atlanta in 1864 still (4) *stirs deep anger in* some Southerners whose forebears remember the fiery havoc created by General William T. Sherman and his troops in their infamous march to the sea. Because Atlanta had been the chief supplier of Confederate munitions, the firing of machine shops and ammunition warehouses turned the (5) *vast and destructive fire* into a nightmare of (6) *fireworks display*.

1. _____   4. _____

2. _____   5. _____

3. _____   6. _____

LESSON 12

*Amicus magis necessarium quam ignis aut aqua.**
A friend is more necessary than fire or water.

KEY WORDS

confluence	hydrology	pontiff
cormorant	inundate	pontificate
dehydrate	marinade	redound
effluent	nauseate	redundant
flux	nave	undulate

---

*The Latin word *ignis*, "fire," appears in the English words *ignite* and *ignition*; the Latin word *aqua*, "water," appears in the English words *aquarium*, *aquatic*, and *aqueduct*.

| **Familiar Words** |
| affluent |
| fluctuate |
| fluent |
| fluid |
| fluorescent |
| fluoridate |
| influence |
| influenza |
| influx |
| mellifluous |
| superfluous |

| **Challenge Words** |
| flume |
| fluor |
| fluvial |
| fluxion |

FLUO, FLUERE, FLUXI, FLUCTUM <L. "to flow"

1. **confluence**   (kŏn´ floo əns)
   [*con* = *cum* <L. "with"]
   n. 1. The flowing together of two or more elements: streams or rivers, or ideas, influences, or cultures.

   If you visit the city of Khartoum in the Sudan, you can stand on a sandbar at the **confluence** of two rivers, the blue Blue Nile and the green White Nile.

   2. An assembling or flocking together in a crowd.

   The **confluence** of flamingos made the air shimmer with the vermilion brilliance of their plumage.

   confluent, *adj.*

2. **effluent**   (ĕf´ loo ənt)   [*e* = *ex* <L. "from," "out of"]
   n. A stream or overflow from a larger body of water, or from a channel or sewer.

   The Environmental Protection Agency has protested the release of hazardous manufacturing **effluents** into the Great Lakes.

   adj. Flowing out.

   An **effluent** vapor floated above the train as it steamed across the prairie.

   effluence, *n.*

3. **flux**   (flŭx)
   n. 1. A flow.

   On the Icelandic island of Heimaey, the **flux** of lava improved the harbor for fishing boats.

   2. A continuous succession of changes.

   The **flux** of drought and civil war in the Horn of Africa has caused millions of people to leave their homes.

| **Familiar Words** |
| hydrant |
| hydroelectric |
| hydrogen |
| hydrophobia |

HUDOR <G. "water"

4. **dehydrate**   (dē hī´ drāt)   [*de* <L. "away from"]
   tr. v. To remove water or moisture.

   To preserve the fruit, the pickers **dehydrated** it on racks open to the sun.

intr. v. To lose water or moisture.

The camel **dehydrates** more slowly than any other animal because it is cud-chewing and makes use of moisture in any form.

dehydrated, *adj.*; **dehydration**, *n.*; **dehydrator**, *n.*

5. **hydrology** (hī drŏl´ ə jē) [*logos* <G. "word," "study"]
n. The study of water and its effects on and in the earth and in the atmosphere.

The Anasazi understood the **hydrology** of the dry Southwest: they built on a plateau, where rain is more plentiful than at lower elevations.

hydrologic, *adj.*; **hydrologist**, *n.*

MAR, MARIS <L. "sea"
MARINUS <L. "marine"

6. **cormorant** (kôr´ mər ənt) [*cor = corvus* <L. "raven"]
n. 1. A dark, hook-billed sea bird.

Chinese villagers on the River Li put collars around the necks of **cormorants** on a leash so that they can dive for fish but not swallow them.

2. A greedy person.

The entrepreneur became a **cormorant** in his drive for wealth.

7. **marinade** (măr´ ə nād)
n. A liquid often seasoned with spices or herbs to flavor meat or fish for a period of time before cooking.

In Madrid, try bullfighter's steak (*caldera de toro*), soaked for four hours in a **marinade** of olive oil flavored with orange, lemon, garlic, cloves, and bay leaf.

marinate, *v.*

NAUS <G. "ship"
NAVIS <L. "ship"
NAUTES <G. "sailor"
NAUTA <L. "sailor"

8. **nauseate** (nô´ zē āt, nô´ zhē āt)
tr. v. 1. To cause queasiness; to cause to feel sick.

The tossing of the ferry boat combined with the smell of frying fish **nauseated** all of the passengers.

Challenge Words
aeronaut
aquanaut
Argonaut
nacelle
navicular

2. To cause the feeling of repulsion or disgust.

Incessant gunfire and exploding cars **nauseate** many moviegoers.

nausea, *n.*; **nauseated**, *adj.*

NOTA BENE: Don't confuse *nauseated* with *nauseous*, which means "causing nausea, the feeling of needing to vomit," and "disgusting or repulsive." To say "I am *nauseous*" means "I make people sick," or "I am disgusting!"

9. nave   (nāv)

n. The long central part of a church, extending from the entrance to the altar, with aisles along the sides.

Because Scandinavian builders were experienced in ship construction, the **naves** of their early churches often resembled a ship's hull turned upside down.

PONS, PONTIS <L. "bridge"

Familiar Word
pontoon

10. pontiff   (pŏn´ tĭf)
n. A pope or bishop.

When the College of Cardinals meets in closed council to elect a new **pontiff**, white smoke rises from the Vatican to announce that it has made a decision.

pontifical, *adj.*

Challenge Words
pons
pons asinorum
pontifex
Pontifex Maximus
pontine
punt
transpontine

11. pontificate   (pŏn tĭf´ ĭ kāt)
intr. v. To speak with pompous authority. (As a verb, **pontificate** also means "to officiate as a pontiff.")

When asked his favorite word learned from scholarly Buffalo Bills coach Mark Levy, a linebacker replied, "**Pontificate**. . . . He **pontificates** for 15 minutes on how he isn't going to **pontificate**."*

n. (pŏn tĭf´ ə kĭt) The office of a pontiff; papacy.

Between 1378 and 1417, the time of the Great Schism, rival **pontificates** in Rome and Avignon claimed authority.

pontification, *n.*

---

*In a *New York Times* article before the 1991 Super Bowl game in Tampa, Florida, sports columnist Ira Berkow described Mark Levy's verbal style and quoted linebacker Ray Bentley, who likes the word *pontificate*. Used with kind permission of the author.

Familiar Words abound abundance superabundant surround

Challenge Word ondine

UNDA <L. "wave" (lit. "a wave of the sea")

12. **undulate** (ŭn´ jōō lāt, ŭn´ dyə lāt, ŭn´ də lāt)
tr. and *intr. v.* To have or to cause to have a wavy motion.

"The ripe corn under the undulating air **undulates** like an ocean." —Percy Bysshe Shelley

undulant, *adj.*; **undulation**, *n.*

13. **redound** (rĭ dound´) [*re* <L. "back," "again"]
intr. v. To reflect or come back either favorably or unfavorably (upon a person or thing).

Election to the National Academy of Sciences in 1944 **redounded** in public recognition of Barbara McClintock's self-effacing brilliance as a geneticist.

14. **redundant** (rĭ dŭn´ dənt) [*re* <L. "back," "again"]
adj. 1. Superfluous; exceeding what is needed, or what is needed no longer.

The invention of electricity made the kerosene lamp **redundant** as a household necessity.

2. Verbose; needlessly repetitious.

The phrase "winning victory" is **redundant**.

redundancy, *n.*

15. **inundate** (ĭn´ ən dāt) [*in* <L. "in"]
tr. v. 1. To submerge or overflow with water; to flood.

According to Genesis, after rain **inundated** the earth for forty days, God offered Noah a covenant, symbolized by the rainbow.

2. To overwhelm.

A crunch of school, job, and family responsibilities can sometimes **inundate** even the best-organized student.

EXERCISE 12A

Circle the letter of the best SYNONYM for the word in bold-faced type.

1. a **nauseating** description   a. sickening   b. graphic   c. pleasing
   d. redounding   e. fervid
2. a favorite **marinade**   a. sea view   b. scented bath   c. water sport
   d. seaside promenade   e. seasoned liquid

3. an expert in **hydrology**   a. sea literature   b. water science
   c. undersea life   d. waterskiing   e. waterworks

4. an impressive **nave**   a. deck of a ship   b. central part of a church
   c. dishonest fellow   d. damp cave   e. church roof

5. **redounds** to your credit   a. contributes   b. disappears
   c. undulates   d. imputes   e. subscribes

6. the international role of a **pontiff**   a. peacemaker   b. genius
   c. bridge-builder   d. pope   e. pastor

Circle the letter of the best ANTONYM for the word in bold-faced type.

7. perpetual **flux**   a. change   b. conflict   c. confluence   d. sanction
   e. constancy

8. the **undulating** sea   a. motionless   b. redounding   c. nauseating
   d. undertowing   e. inundating

9. a sudden **inundation** of honors   a. effluence   b. ether   c. drought
   d. conflagration   e. apogee

EXERCISE 12B

Circle the letter of the sentence in which the word in bold-faced type is used incorrectly.

1. a. Don't let that old **cormorant** overcharge you for your room.
   b. Along the salt marshes **cormorants** were feeding on small fish.
   c. If you hadn't been so **cormorant**, everyone could have had second helpings of dessert.
   d. In South America **cormorants** are a valuable source of guano, or dung, which is used as a fertilizer.

2. a. Many in the **flux** of refugees escaping from Vietnam by boat were beset by starvation and dehydration.
   b. Embarrassment **fluxes** their faces a bright red.
   c. The natural **flux** of the eye's fluids keeps it purified.
   d. Popular fads are always in **flux**: dozens of dance crazes appeared between the Big Apple in the 1930s and the Bunny Hop in the 1950s.

3. a. Bridges and aqueducts **pontificated** by Roman builders remain throughout Europe.
   b. Successful executives do more than simply **pontificate** about running their companies efficiently; they work with employees and introduce ways to eradicate waste.
   c. From the publication of her first book on etiquette, Emily Post **pontificated** on rules of proper behavior in every conceivable social situation.
   d. Although his **pontificate** lasted only five years, John XXIII earned world-wide esteem for his words on justice and peace among nations.

4. a. We managed to reduce my **redundant** article to three pages.

b. A combination of languages in place names can create **redundancies**; Los Altos Hills means "Hills Hills," and Lake Lagunita, "Lake Little Lake."

c. Will the word processor ever make the typewriter completely **redundant**?

d. Weight control programs and low-calorie frozen dinners appeal to people with a **redundancy** of pounds.

5. a. Accomplished divers leave hardly a ripple at their point of **inundation**.

b. Although the Aswan Dam **inundated** many villages and historical sites and forced relocation of thousands of people, control of flooding on the Nile River now makes land available all year around.

c. The forces that **inundated** the now legendary island of Atlantis have remained a tantalizing mystery for centuries.

d. As more women take jobs, they also feel **inundated** with competing responsibilities of home and family.

6. a. In a summer of heavy rains, flooding occurs when the Missouri and Mississippi Rivers rush to their **confluence** north of Saint Louis.

b. The concert was a success because of a **confluence** of factors: the brilliant young violinist Midori, her resonant instrument, and the inspired conductor.

c. At the auction of Greta Garbo's art collection, a **confluence** of movie fans and art connoisseurs acknowledged her discerning taste.

d. Although the **confluence** of the Rio Grande swells in the rainy season, it can narrow to a muddy stream in summer.

7. a. Hikers concerned about **dehydration** should remember that carbohydrates produce both water and energy more readily than other food groups.

b. The creature least likely to become **dehydrated** is the kangaroo rat of the Southwest; once weaned, it never needs to drink again.

c. We spent some blissful **dehydrating** hours swimming in the ocean.

d. In regions affected by famine and drought, **dehydration** is a frequent cause of death, especially among infants.

8. a. For more than thirty-five years an **effluent** containing mercury has been causing illness and death in the Japanese city of Minamata.

b. Parents are protesting the **effluence** on children when television cartoon characters become toys for sale during commercial breaks.

c. The **effluence** from the conservatory practice rooms was a wild cacophony of singers, cellos, clarinets, and drums.

      d. At first a mystery, Legionnaire's disease was traced to an **effluent** from air conditioners in a Philadelphia hotel.

9. a. Let the shrimp soak in a **marinade** of olive oil and lemon juice before you cook it.

      b. The hairdresser keeps a complete line of **marinades** in stock for customers who like to change their hair color.

      c. The columnist Russell Baker has written that he has been intending to "**marinate**" himself in all of the arts so that he will be as cognizant of those subjects as any know-it-all reviewer.

      d. According to the chef Julia Child, a cook **marinates** meat but *macerates* fruit, soaking it in liquid.

EXERCISE 12C   Fill in each blank with the most appropriate word from the following word list. Use a word only once.

confluence	*hudor*	nave	redounds
cormorant	hydrologists	*pons*	redundant
dehydration	*mar*	pontiff	*unda*
effluent	nauseate	pontificate	undulation

1. The commentator Harry Reasoner once reprimanded a staff writer for using the word _____ instead of the simpler word *pope*.

2. A word that can be either a noun or an adjective and means "outflowing" is _____.

3. Film and television stars often discover that celebrity _____ in loss of privacy.

4. _____ have calculated that only three percent of the world's water supply is fresh, and most of that exists in icebergs.

5. A physician studies the patterns of _____ on an electrocardiogram to determine the health of the patient's heart as it contracts and relaxes.

6. An English noun coming from the Latin word for "ship" suggests a metaphorical connection with a church; the word is _____.

7. When speaking to an audience large or small, try not to _____ unless you really know what you are talking about.

8. If you tell someone you are majoring in water hydrology, you are _____.

9. The Ganges and the Jumna, the two holy rivers of India, have their point of _____ at Allahabad.

10. The black bird with green eyes, webbed feet, and a hooked bill, to be found on both Atlantic and Pacific coasts, is probably a(n)

_____.

11. The three Latin or Greek words that are most likely to get you

soaking wet are _____, _____,

and _____.

12. Experts say that if you are adrift at sea for many days, you may

limit _____ by (1) keeping your clothing wet with seawater and (2) eating raw fish livers.

13. The word most likely to express your reaction to a fact mentioned

in sentence 12 is _____.

EXERCISE 12D   Each word in italics can have more than one meaning. Write the meaning of the word implied by the context of the paragraph.

Located at the point where Europe meets Asia, Istanbul has long been the point of (1) *confluence* for many cultures. Its architecture reflects the (2) *flux* of civilizations that have flourished on this peninsula. The domed sixth-century basilica of Hagia Sophia, consecrated in 537 during the (3) *pontificate* of Pope Virgilius, recalls the period when, as Constantinople, the city was the eastern capital of the late Roman Empire and later, as Byzantium, the center of an isolated and shrinking realm that was eventually (4) *inundated* by advancing Muslim armies.

1. _____   3. _____

2. _____   4. _____

REVIEW EXERCISES FOR LESSONS 11 AND 12

1

Circle the letter of the best answer.

1. cauterize : burn : :
   a. inundate : dry
   b. nauseate : travel
   c. pontificate : shout
   d. effervesce : bubble
   e. redound : jump
2. redound : *unda* : :
   a. pontiff : *pur*
   b. incense : *kaiein*
   c. flagrant : *flamma*
   d. flamboyant : *flagrare*
   e. hydrology : *hudor*

2 Matching: On the lines at the left, write the letters of the literal (concrete) and metaphorical definitions of each word.

Concrete   Metaphorical

_____ _____ **1.** dehydration

_____ _____ **2.** pyrotechnics

_____ _____ **3.** inundation

_____ _____ **4.** cormorant

_____ _____ **5.** effervescence

A. brilliance
B. drying out
C. a miser
D. excitement
E. flood
F. fireworks
G. lack of inspiration
H. a bird
I. bubbles
J. crush

3 Sentence completion: Choose the adjective from the list below that best describes the situation in the sentence, and write the word in the blank.

1. If you deliberately violate a traffic law by running a red light, you are _____.
2. If you talk about a "free gift" and use other words you don't need, you are _____.
3. If you wear your new purple sweater with red, orange, and green squares, you are

   _____.
4. If you think you know everything about the innards of automobiles and become dogmatic you

   are _____.
5. If you attend every game your team plays and attach its logo to all of your clothing you are

   _____.
6. If you take a ride on a rollercoaster and feel very queasy, you are _____.
7. If you are furious when a friend fails to return your book the night before the big test, you are

   _____.
8. If you join two other students to publish a multicultural newspaper, your interests are

   _____.
9. If you sometimes hurt people with your sarcasm and biting wit, you are _____.
10. If you are known as "Bubbles" by your friends because of your high spirits, you are

   _____.

caustic
confluent
effervescent
fervid
flagrant
flamboyant
incensed
nauseated
pontificating
redundant

4 Writing or Discussion Activities

1. a. When a fictional character makes a decision and acts upon it, something important often happens. Whether the character makes demands upon other characters, commits a blunder, delivers an ultimatum, or simply does nothing, the decision has probably had consequences that *redound* positively or negatively upon that person. Choose from your reading a situation in which something has redounded, and write a paragraph explaining the specific decision, action, and consequences affecting that character. Some books that supply examples are *A Separate Peace, The Chosen, A Member of the Wedding, Annie John, Of Mice and Men,* and *The Summer of My German Soldier.*

b. In a second paragraph, write about an important decision that you yourself have made, and describe the redounding effects of it. Explain your decision, the subsequent action, and the results: satisfying, unsatisfying, or mixed? surprising? painful? gratifying? inevitable?

2. As you look at the following list of adjectives, what real or imaginary people come to mind?

flamboyant	incendiary
caustic	pontificating
scintillating	fervid
inundated	incensed

Choose two adjectives that apply to two people or characters, and write a dialogue in which your speakers show the quality that represents each of them. Involve your pair in one or more specific situations. You may discover a cause-and-effect relationship between the words chosen; for example, an *incendiary* remark from one person may incite a *caustic* reply from the other.

Order and Disorder in the Universe

LESSON 13

Non est ad astra mollis a terris via.
The way from the earth to the stars is not easy.—SENECA

Key Words

apostle	cosmopolite	ordinance
asterisk	epistolary	rectify
astral	inordinate	rectitude
constellation	insubordinate	stellar
cosmology	ordain	stolid

Familiar Words
coordinate
disorder
extraordinary
ordinary
primordial
subordinate

ORDO, ORDINIS <L. "order," "series," "row," "line"

1. **insubordinate**   (ĭn´sə bôrd´ n ĭt)
   [*in* <L. "not"]
   adj. Not submissive to authority.

   When the desperately hungry Oliver Twist says, "Please, sir, more" tasteless gruel, he is punished by the schoolmaster for what is considered **insubordinate** behavior.

   insubordination, *n.*

111

2. **inordinate** (ĭn ôrd´ n ĭt) [*in* <L. "not"]
adj. Excessive; immoderate; not controlled.

Pandora's **inordinate** curiosity led her to open a forbidden box from which escaped all earthly plagues, and only hope was left inside.

3. **ordain** (ôr dān´)
tr. v. 1. To confirm priestly authority upon.

Reform Jewish congregations in the United States now **ordain** women as rabbis.

2. To order by superior authority.

Congress **ordained** that the third Monday in January would honor the birthday of Martin Luther King, Jr., the civil rights leader slain in 1968.

ordination, *n.*

4. **ordinance** (ôrd´ n əns)
n. 1. A command or order; a law or regulation, especially by a city government.

In 1944 a Mexican **ordinance** abolished the siesta, the practice of closing businesses and offices during midday hours.

2. A custom or practice established by tradition, especially a religious rite.

A Muslim **ordinance** requires that believers fast between sunrise and sunset during the holy month of Ramadan.

STELLEIN <G. "to put," "to place"

5. **apostle** (ə pŏs´ əl) [*apo* <G. "away from"]
n. A leader or teacher of a (new) faith or movement. (When capitalized, *Apostle* refers to one of twelve men sent forth by Jesus to spread his teachings.)

With her 1962 book, *Silent Spring*, Rachel Carson became an **apostle** of environmental protection, warning against chemicals toxic to the earth and its creatures.

Apostolic, *adj.*; **apostolic**, *adj.*

6. **stolid** (stŏl´ ĭd)
adj. Showing or appearing to feel no emotion; apathetic.

Elizabeth Cady Stanton has written that "history shows that the masses of all oppressed classes . . . have been **stolid** and apathetic until partial success had crowned the faith and enthusiasm of the few."

7. **epistolary**   (ĭ pĭs´ tə lĕr´ ē)   [*epi* <G. "on"]
adj. Pertaining to letter-writing or contained in letters.

In one of many **epistolary** exchanges from France with her sister, Abigail Adams observed that "fashion is the deity everyone worships in this country."

epistle, *n.*; **Epistle**, *n.*

REGO, REGERE, REXI, RECTUM <L. "to guide," "to govern"

8. **rectify**   (rĕk´ tə fī)   [*-fy* = *facere* <L. "to make"]
tr. v. To set right; to correct.

Through Ada Deer's advocacy, the U.S. government in 1973 returned forest land to the Menominee people and **rectified** an earlier transfer of the land to the state of Wisconsin.

9. **rectitude**   (rĕk´ tə tōōd, rĕk´ tə tyōōd)
n. Moral uprightness; correctness of behavior.

According to Jewish legend, the presence of at least thirty-six righteous men in every generation will provide **rectitude** enough to justify the survival of the world.

NOTA BENE: Some words derived from *luna*, "moon," are probably already familiar to you: *lunar* and *lunatic*, the latter suggesting the influence of the moon as a cause of insanity. *Sublunary* means "beneath the moon," or "terrestrial," and *superlunary*, "above the moon," or "celestial."

STELLA <L. "star"

10. **constellation**   (kŏn´stə lā´ shən)   [*con* = *cum* <L. "with"]
n. 1. A group of fixed stars.

Ancient Chinese, Egyptian, and Mesopotamian astronomers divided the stars into groups of **constellations** whose pictorial representations resemble some signs of the zodiac.

2. A brilliant gathering.

A **constellation** of eighteenth-century politicians, artists, actors, and writers, David Garrick and Samuel Johnson among them, belonged to The Club, which met regularly in a London inn.

Familiar Words
correct
direct
erect
realm
rectangle
rectum
regime
regiment
region
regular
regulate
surge

Challenge Words
rectilinear
recto
rector
risorgimento

Familiar Words
Stella
Estella

Challenge Words
stellate
stelliform
stellify

3. A set of related objects or individuals.

At the Turkish market, flatwoven rugs called *kilims* were **constellations** of ancient symbolic designs in rich colors.

constellate, *v.*

11. **stellar**   (stěl´ ər)
adj. 1. Pertaining to stars.

With the discovery of **stellar** spectra, colors produced by hot gases and measured in wavelengths, astronomers are able to ascertain the chemical composition of stars.

2. Outstanding; referring to a star performer.

In Chile, Conchita Cintrón was recognized as a **stellar** bullfighter.

ASTER <G. and L. "star"

Familiar Words
asteroid
astrology
astronomical
astronomy
disaster

12. **asterisk**   (ăs´ tə rĭsk)
n. A star-shaped figure used to indicate an omission or a footnote.

Use **asterisks** to alert your reader to one (*) or two (**) notes at the foot of a page; for more notes, use numbers.

13. **astral**   (ăs´ trəl)
adj. Of or from the stars.

Using his great quadrant and naked eye for **astral** and planetary sightings, Tycho Brahe became the foremost sixteenth-century astronomer in the Western world.

Challenge Words
asterism
astrocyte
astrobiology
astrophysics
astrosphere

NOTA BENE: Although *astral* and *stellar* can sometimes be synonyms, as in *astral* or *stellar* light, *stellar* has more variations of meaning, often metaphorically, as the phrase "stellar performance" illustrates.

KOSMOS <G. "universe"

Familiar Words
cosmetic
cosmonaut
cosmos
macrocosm
microcosm

14. **cosmology**   (kŏz mŏl´ ə jē)   [*logos* <G. "word," "study"]
n. The study of the whole universe: origin, evolution, and relationship of its parts.

The dimensions of **cosmology** have grown vastly as satellite photographs probe ever deeper among galaxies beyond the Milky Way.

Challenge Words
cosmogenic
cosmogony
cosmography

15. cosmopolite (kŏz mŏp´ ə līt)
[*polis* <G. "city"]
n. A person at ease in any part of the world and/or knowledgeable in many subjects.

Lee Miller, a **cosmopolite** who spent most of her life abroad, achieved success as a fashion model, war reporter, and photographer.

cosmopolis, *n.*; **cosmopolitan**, *adj.*

EXERCISE 13A   Circle the letter of the best SYNONYM for the word in bold-faced type.

1. Dimmesdale's apparent **rectitude**   a. rigidity   b. passivity
   c. corrupt behavior   d. virtuousness   e. carelessness
2. their **inordinate** thrift   a. moderate   b. excessive   c. genuine
   d. rash   e. flamboyant
3. a(n) **stellar** audience   a. cognizant   b. attentive   c. ordinary
   d. truly remarkable   e. well-dressed
4. to **rectify** the situation   a. relax   b. organize   c. correct
   d. change   e. corrupt
5. **asterisks** in the text   a. periods   b. concave-convex shapes
   c. star-shaped figures   d. asteroids   e. configurations

Circle the letter of the best ANTONYM for the word in bold-faced type.

6. a weary **cosmopolite**   a. mountebank   b. urbanite   c. scholar
   d. foreigner   e. rustic
7. **apostles** of technology   a. distributers   b. students   c. witnesses
   d. opponents   e. buyers
8. **insubordinate** employees   a. nervous   b. dispirited
   c. cooperative   d. incendiary   e. hyperbolic
9. a **stolid** manner   a. weak   b. resolute   c. sycophantic   d. mild
   e. passionate
10. to **ordain** a peaceful transition   a. expect   b. reject   c. pledge
    d. discuss   e. demand
11. a(n) **astral** phenomenon   a. terrestrial   b. ethereal
    c. flamboyant   d. redundant   e. inanimate

EXERCISE 13B   Circle the letter of the sentence in which the word in bold-faced type is used incorrectly.

1. a. Many cities have established an **ordinance** against smoking in public places.
   b. After their **ordinance**, the class officers held their first meeting.
   c. **Ordinances** called "Blue Laws," forbidding work on the Sabbath, developed from puritanical restraints initiated by seventeenth-century religious zealots.
   d. Church **ordinances** now allow girls as well as boys to serve as acolytes.

2. a. The nomenclature of **constellations** commemorates characters in Greek myths, such as Andromeda, Hercules, and Orion followed by the dog Sirius.
   b. New Yorkers remember with **constellation** the night in 1965 when the entire city went black after electric power failed.
   c. During a quarter of a century a **constellation** of Soong family members—a son and three daughters—significantly influenced the political life of China.
   d. For art lovers the city of Florence represents a **constellation** of Renaissance architecture, sculpture, and painting.

3. a. Many early novels were **epistolary**, revealing a character's innermost thoughts and actions through letters he or she writes.
   b. Observations in St. Paul's **Epistle** to the Galatians inspired Martin Luther in molding the Protestant Reformation.
   c. A character in a novel by Mavis Gallant offers this **epistolary** advice: "Don't cry whilst writing letters. . . . If you must tell the world about your personal affairs, give examples. Don't just sob in the pillow hoping someone will hear."
   d. Ralph Nader's role as consumer watchdog has had an **epistolary** effect upon prices and services in the last two decades.

4. a. Receiving the 1945 Nobel Prize for Literature gave the Chilean poet Gabriela Mistral a **stellar** place among South American writers.
   b. Her 1986 performance in *Children of a Lesser God* made Marlee Matlin a **stellar** and won her an Oscar.
   c. In a Washco myth, the wily Coyote seeks applause for his **stellar** handiwork: providing the heavens with five wolf brothers, sky pictures, and a Big Road made from left-over stars.
   d. In ancient times the city of Babylon on the Euphrates River was a **stellar** attraction for its culture and magnificence.

5. a. At the cosmetic counter an eminent **cosmologist** was ready to demonstrate the newest line of creams and colors.
   b. **Cosmologists** generally agree that the big bang theory explains the origin of the universe.

c. According to one expert, Edwin P. Hubble's 1929 discovery that the universe is expanding uniformly in all directions made **cosmology** a genuine science.

d. The mythology of cultures around the world contains stories explaining **cosmological** origins and stellar deities.

6. a. In the epistolary novel *Pamela*, the **rectitude** of the maidservant finally convinces her employer that marriage is the only way he will ever win her.

b. Although labeled an "Enemy of the People" in Henrik Ibsen's play, Dr. Thomas Stockman exemplifies **rectitude** in maintaining truth: the city's spa is contaminated and must be shut down.

c. The winner of the spelling bee has a natural **rectitude** for spelling a word correctly even when she hears it for the first time.

d. In Greek literature two forms of **rectitude** became personified: Nemesis, or righteous anger, and Aidos, feelings that prevent wrongdoing and increase sensitivity to undeserved suffering.

7. a. Stella Gibbons alludes to the proverbial **stolidity** of cows when she writes, "Graceless, Pointless, Feckless and Aimless waited their turn to be milked."

b. Portraits of the former Soviet leader Joseph Stalin show him with a **stolid**, unyielding expression, a man of power, not of compassion.

c. The **stolid** monument known as Cleopatra's Needle stands alongside a busy London thoroughfare on the Thames River Embankment.

d. In Joseph Conrad's *Heart of Darkness*, the protagonist, Marlow, is shocked to see exhausted natives sitting **stolidly** under a tree, shackled and starving.

8. a. Jessye Norman is **cosmopolitan** not only in her travel to cities in the United States and Europe, but also for the many nationalities she assumes in operas.

b. In Baroness Orczy's novel, Sir Percy Blakeney leads the League of the Scarlet Pimpernel, using his **cosmopolitan** finesse to rescue victims of the French Reign of Terror.

c. When Socrates says, "I am not an Athenian nor a Greek, but a citizen of the world," he gives us a definition of **cosmopolite**.

d. Books about geography help you become **cosmopolite**.

9. a. Collectors of antique cars are often willing to pay **astral** prices for a vintage Stanley Steamer or Dusenberg.

b. Including the Sun, the **astral** population of our galaxy, the Milky Way, numbers 100,000.

c. Many primitive peoples have assigned divine powers to **astral** bodies.

d. The aster is a flower that takes its name from an **astral** shape: petals radiating from a yellow center.

EXERCISE 13C   Fill in each blank with the most appropriate word from Lesson 13. Use a word or any of its forms only once.

1. In 1990 Congress _____ that Native American languages would be "encouraged and supported as languages of instruction" in schools.

2. The _____ of Odysseus's greedy crew as they open the crucial bag of winds not only enrages him, but also further delays their return from the Trojan War.

3. Marie-Thérésè Basse, a(n) _____ for relief of food shortages in countries bordering the Sahara, developed a millet that can be locally grown.

4. In *Letters to Alice on First Reading Jane Austen*, Fay Weldon uses a(n)

   _____ format to express her admiration for Austen as a way to help an imaginary niece write her own novel.

5. A(n) _____ may call attention to a note containing details too lengthy for the body of the report.

6. When baseball cards in mint condition are rare and picture stellar

   players, people will pay _____ prices to own them.

7. Until they were rectified in the mid-twentieth century,

   _____ in some states made marriage between whites and nonwhites illegal.

8. According to the astronomer Dr. Allan R. Sandage, advances in

   _____ have moved the study of the universe from ethereal speculation to concrete measurement and record.

9. At an annual awards ceremony at the Kennedy Center, a(n)

   _____ of distinguished performers in the arts receives recognition.

10. Attempting to _____ a historical injustice, a grandson of Dr. Samuel Mudd claims that he was not an accomplice of Abraham Lincoln's assassin, John Wilkes Booth, but only set his leg before letting him go.

EXERCISE 13D   Replace the word or phrase in italics with a key word (or any of its forms) from Lesson 13.

Founded in 1848 by Dante Gabriel Rossetti, the Pre-Raphaelite Brotherhood was a (1) *brilliant group* of mid-nineteenth-century artists joined to (2) *correct* the state of British art by returning to principles of Italian art before Raphael in the sixteenth century. The (3) *leaders* of this artistic movement (4) *decreed* the faithful representation of beauty in everyday life, which they depicted with meticulous detail and brilliant color. Another of the brotherhood's (5) *dicta* was infusion of spirituality, often accomplished by using subject matter from history, mythology, and literature. The (6) *outstanding* figures who founded the Pre-Raphaelite movement, Dante Gabriel Rossetti, W. Holman Hunt, and John Millais, attracted notable artists like Edward Coley Burne-Jones and William Morris.

1. _____   4. _____

2. _____   5. _____

3. _____   6. _____

LESSON 14

Mutatis mutandis.
Things having been changed that had to be changed.

Key Words		
aspersion	penultimate	temper
disperse	permutation	temperance
immutable	perturb	transmute
imperturbable	temerarious	turbid
outré	temerity	ultimatum

Familiar Words
commute
mutable
mutant
mutation

MUTO, MUTARE, MUTAVI, MUTATUM <L. "to change"

1. **immutable** (ĭ myoot´ ə bəl) [*im* = *in* <L. "not"]
   adj. Never changing or varying; unchangeable.

   Alice James believed in "the **immutable** law that however great we may seem in our own consciousness no human being would exchange his for ours."

2. **permutation** (pûr´myoo tā´ shən) [*per* <L. "through"]
   n. An alteration; a rearrangement of elements, especially in mathematics.

   Mathematical **permutation** may alter the sequence of symbols in a group, as in *xy* to *yx*.

   permute, *v.*

3. **transmute** (trăns myoot´, trănz myoot´) [*trans* <L. "across"]
   tr. v. To transform; to change from one form of nature into another.

In a Guatemalan legend, Brother Pedro **transmutes** a green lizard into an emerald so that the penniless Juan may prosper; when secure, Juan returns the gem, which the monk **transmutes** to its original form.

transmutation, *n.*

TEMERITAS <L. "rashness," "thoughtlessness"

4. temerity (tə měr´ ĭ tē)
n. Foolish boldness; recklessness; rashness.

As Daedalus and his son escape from Crete on handmade wings, Icarus has the **temerity** to fly so high that the sun melts the wax, and he falls to his death in the sea.

5. temerarious (těm´ ə râr´ ē əs)
adj. Daring; rash; reckless.

One of the original photographers for *Life* magazine, Marguerite Bourke-White proved **temerarious** and intrepid with her camera in military zones during World War II and the Korean War.

temerariousness, *n.*

TURBO, TURBARE, TURBAVI, TURBATUM <L. "to disturb," "to throw into disorder"

6. imperturbable (ĭm´ pər tûr´ bə bəl)
[*im-* = *in* <L. "not"; *per* <L. "through"]
adj. Unexcitable; unflustered; calm.

In the novel *Yellow Raft on Blue Water,* Aunt Ida, despite searing experiences in her life, maintains an **imperturbable** exterior that reflects her Native American heritage.

imperturbability, *n.*

7. turbid (tûr´ bəd)
adj. 1. Muddy; not clear; opaque.

When oil wells burn, they release **turbid,** toxic smoke that threatens human and plant life in an entire region.

2. Confused; disordered.

According to Walter Savage Landor, "Clear writers, like clear fountains, do not seem so deep as they are; the **turbid** look the most profound."

NOTA BENE: Avoid confusing *turbid* with *turgid*, which means "swollen" or "bloated," as a snake's condition might be after swallowing a mouse. *Turgid* can also mean *bloated* in another sense: someone's style of writing may be too ornate or grandiose, and therefore be considered *turgid*.

8. perturb (pər tûrb´) [*per* <L. "through"]
tr. v. To agitate; to upset.

Letters to the editor increase when issues such as police brutality and harm to the environment **perturb** newspaper readers.

perturbation, *n*.; **perturbed**, *adj.*

Familiar Words
intersperse
spark
sparkle
sparse
sprinkle

Challenge Word
asperges

SPARGO, SPARGERE, SPARSI, SPARSUM <L. "to scatter," "to cast," "to sprinkle"

9. aspersion (ə spûr´ zhən, ə spûr´ shən)
[*a* = *ad* <L. "to," "toward"]
n. A remark that disparages, maligns, or slanders another.

Some universities have proscribed deliberate **aspersions** that insult or degrade persons on the basis of race, sex, or nationality.

asperse, *v.*

10. disperse (dĭs pûrs´) [*dis* <L. "apart"]
tr. v. To spread widely; to disseminate.

During the Civil War, Union troops **dispersed** leaflets throughout the countryside to encourage their Confederate opponents to surrender.

tr. and *intr. v.* To scatter; to dispel; to drive away.

Some airports use recordings of gunfire to **disperse** seagulls that gather on runways, presenting a hazard for departing jets.

dispersal, *n*.; **dispersion**, *n.*

Familiar Words
tamper
temperament
temperature

TEMPERO, TEMPERARE, TEMPERAVI, TEMPERATUM <L. "to combine in proportion"

11. temper (tĕm´ pər)
tr. v. 1. To moderate.

Joseph Addison, an eighteenth-century essayist, declared, "I shall endeavor to enliven morality with wit, and to **temper** wit with morality."

2. To bring to a particular texture or consistency, often hardness.

The manufacturer of fine knives **tempers** the steel to the degree of hardness that will best keep the blade sharp.

NOTA BENE: You are already familiar with the use of the noun *temper* to mean "an outburst of anger." *Temper* can also be a neutral word meaning "mood" or "temperament," as in "Poodles are known for their even *temper*."

12. **temperance** (tĕm´ pər əns)
n. 1. Moderation in expressing feelings, in appetite, and in consumption of alcoholic drink; self-restraint.

According to the Roman orator Cicero, "**Temperance** is the moderating of one's desires in obedience to reason."

2. Total abstinence from alcoholic beverages; teetotalism.

In the cause of **temperance** Carry Nation and her crusaders marched into saloons, singing hymns and swinging hatchets.

temperate, *adj.*

Antonym: **intemperance**

<table>
<tr><td>

Familiar Words
ultimate
ultraconservative
ultrahigh
  frequency
ultramodern
ultraviolet rays

</td></tr>
</table>

<table>
<tr><td>

Challenge Words
ultima Thule
ultramarine
ultramontane
ultrasonic

</td></tr>
</table>

ULTIMO, ULTIMARE <L. "to come to the end," "to be last"
ULTRA <L. "beyond"

13. **outré** (o͞o trā´)
adj. Deviating from the usual or proper; eccentric; outlandish.

In 1910 a dress revealing an ankle was thought **outré**.

14. **penultimate** (pĭ nŭl´ tə mĭt) [*pen = paena* <L. "almost"]
adj. Next to last.

On January 3, 1959, Alaska became the **penultimate** state in the Union, followed in the same year by Hawaii.

penult, *n.*

15. **ultimatum** (ŭl´ tə mā´ təm, ŭl´ tə mä´ təm; plural **ultimatums** or **ultimata**: ŭl´ tə mā tə)
n. A final, uncompromising condition or demand, especially one whose rejection will close negotiations.

When Juliet refuses to wed Count Paris, her father issues an **ultimatum** to marry or nevermore be acknowledged as his daughter.

EXERCISE 14A Circle the letter of the best SYNONYM for the word in bold-faced type.

1. **perturbing** events   a. worrisome   b. confusing   c. calming
   d. maturing   e. interesting
2. **turbid** election results   a. challenged   b. clearcut   c. irregular
   d. delayed   e. muddled
3. a habit of **temerity**   a. bravery   b. ostentation   c. confidence
   d. rashness   e. carefulness
4. to **temper** selfish motives   a. control   b. rationalize   c. condone
   d. deny   e. respect
5. **immutable** conditions   a. complex   b. sacrosanct   c. durable
   d. fluctuating   e. unchangeable
6. the **penultimate** chapter   a. last   b. next-to-last   c. second
   d. altered   e. unchanged

Circle the letter of the best ANTONYM for the word in bold-faced type.

7. **outré** remarks   a. commonplace   b. cruel   c. notorious
   d. turbid   e. original
8. a plea for **temperance**   a. pacifism   b. justice   c. frugality
   d. calm   e. prodigality
9. a predictable **transmutation**   a. alteration   b. impediment
   c. immutability   d. analogy   e. modification
10. **dispersal** of property   a. retention   b. distribution
    c. improvement   d. deterioration   e. selling
11. unjustified **aspersions**   a. slanders   b. compliments
    c. confluences   d. declamations   e. valedictions

EXERCISE 14B Circle the letter of the sentence in which the word in bold-faced type is used incorrectly.

1. a. Because the Ganges River is considered holy, throngs coming to
      bathe in it keep it **turbid**.
   b. In his essay "Politics and the English Language" George Orwell
      attacks prose made **turbid** by redundancy and verbosity.
   c. During wartime when soldiers stand in mud or water for long
      periods of time, they often suffer from trenchfoot, which causes
      painful and debilitating **turbidity**.
   d. Dredging rivers to control the growth of water hyacinths keeps
      the water **turbid** with silt.

2. a. During the Vietnam War in the 1960s, protesting students often issued **ultimata** demanding that their university cease war-related research.

   b. The scavenger-hunt winners found both the penultimate and **ultimatum** items required: a live snake and a French franc.

   c. According to the Bible, Lot's wife does not heed the **ultimatum** to leave Sodom and Gomorrah without looking back and is turned into a pillar of salt for her insubordination.

   d. The gods delivered an **ultimatum** to Thebes—the murderer of King Laius must be brought to justice or the plague will continue.

3. a. In her single-engine plane, Beryl Markham **temerariously** delivered mail and rescued downed pilots in remote regions of Kenya.

   b. Made famous in a poem by Alfred, Lord Tennyson, the British Charge of the Light Brigade in 1854 was a **temerarious** and costly assault on Russian troops at Balaclava during the Crimean War.

   c. **Temerarious** review of information before a test guarantees that students are fully prepared to perform creditably.

   d. The actor Errol Flynn typically played **temerarious** heroes in such films as *Captain Blood* and *Beau Geste*.

4. a. Although Mr. Micawber declines into poverty that sends him and his family to debtor's prison, he remains **imperturbable**, always sure that "something will turn up."

   b. Some people have so little sense of direction that they become **imperturbably** confused when trying to follow a road map.

   c. When Gulliver visits Laputa, he cannot believe the **imperturbability** of citizens whose attention must be caught by servants rattling flappers on sticks.

   d. Despite reporters' challenging questions, the president's spokesperson remained **imperturbable** throughout her White House press conferences.

5. a. Since the formation of national baseball teams in 1857, rules of the sport have undergone many **permutations**.

   b. As Alice visits Wonderland, she experiences surprising **permutations**, growing into a giant and shrinking to insect size.

   c. In *The Odyssey* the sorceress Circe **permutes** members of Odysseus's crew into pigs.

   d. That dress went through several **permutations**, from Mother's prom gown to my dress-up costume to quilt squares.

6. a. In retaliation for his lack of promotion, Iago launches **aspersions** against Othello by challenging the fidelity of his wife.

   b. "My life became a tissue of rumors and accusations," said German filmmaker Leni Riefenstahl when speaking of **aspersions** resulting from her purported involvement with Nazi propaganda.

   c. For many professional dancers, the **aspersion** of dancing as a career begins in childhood.

      d. In his 1950's hunt for Communists in government, Senator Joseph McCarthy cast **aspersions** on many innocent people.

7. a. After much practice, singers of atonal music learn to **temper** their pitch and hit the note the composer intended.

      b. Hard work and a harsh climate **temper** the spirit of Ántonia Shimerda in Willa Cather's novel *My Ántonia.*

      c. At outdoor summer concerts the pure sounds of talented musicians can partially **temper** heat, insect bites, and the thirst of listeners.

      d. The chef **tempered** the soup generously with cloves of garlic and his favorite hot chili peppers.

8. a. Since the first publication of Laurence Sterne's *Tristram Shandy,* readers have found the novel **outré** for its interspersed blank or black or marbled pages and missing or dislocated chapters, all part of the author's scheme.

      b. Because their ideas and their blue worsted stockings were considered **outré**, intellectual women of the 1750s were called "Blue Stockings," still a term of aspersion.

      c. For some diehards in every age, new inventions seem **outré**, even the automobile, the airplane, and the telephone, because they appear to violate traditional modes of travel and communication.

      d. The museum's display featured many **outré** objects: arrowheads and wooden tools.

EXERCISE 14C   Fill in each blank with the most appropriate word from Lesson 14. Use a word or any of its forms only once.

    1. To pronounce the word *constellation* correctly, place the accent on the _____ syllable.

    2. Desperate to outrun her would-be lover Apollo, Daphne escapes him when her father _____ her into a laurel tree.

    3. Don José Artigas, loyal to Simón Bolívar, became an apostle for land rights of the indigenous people, having the _____ to oppose wealthy South American landowners.

    4. Some mathematicians believe in _____ relationships of mathematical elements that seem timeless and valid in all places at all times.

    5. The rainclouds _____ in time for the graduation ceremonies to proceed as planned.

6. An ardent apostle of _____, Evangeline Booth writes that alcohol has "Dug more graves than any other poisoned / Scourge."

7. Because she had tricks up her sleeve to rectify every situation, the effervescent Mary Poppins could remain _____ no matter what problems beset her.

8. _____ of flu viruses occurs so rapidly that a vaccine for one variety becomes useless the following year.

9. When the government failed to respond to their _____ for better working conditions, the air traffic controllers went on strike.

10. Increasing signs of global warming _____ environmentalists, who fear the consequences of greater deterioration of the ozone layer.

11. Some people considered Margaret Mead _____ for going to a remote South Sea island to conduct research in the thirties.

EXERCISE 14D   Replace the word or phrase in italics with a key word (or any of its forms) from Lesson 14.

When the world of high fashion issues a(n) (1) *uncompromising decree*, many people obey, no matter how (2) *"far out"* the command. Casting (3) *insulting remarks* on last year's "look," they (4) *daringly* adorn themselves in this year's "latest thing."

Others follow Alexander Pope's advice to "Be not the first by whom the new is tried,/ Nor yet the last to lay the old aside." Avoiding what they consider the (5) *foolish boldness* of the avant-garde, these people prefer the (6) *next-to-latest* offering to the very latest. They (7) *moderate* last year's high fashion, (8) *altering* it into this year's conservative style.

Still others ignore the (9) *confused* world of fashion altogether. Once they have found what suits them, their taste is (10) *unchangeable*. Fashion (11) *seriously upsets* them only when they cannot find a new jacket or pair of shoes exactly like the old ones.

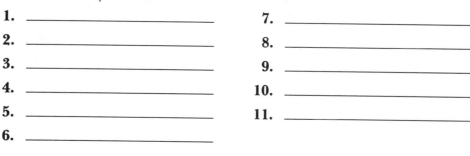

1. _____   7. _____

2. _____   8. _____

3. _____   9. _____

4. _____   10. _____

5. _____   11. _____

6. _____

REVIEW EXERCISES FOR LESSONS 13 AND 14

1 Circle the letter of the most appropriate pair of words to complete the following sentences.

1. By _____ a salesman into an insect, Franz Kafka forces readers of *Metamorphosis* to recognize the _____ pretension and self-interest of family members.
   a. permuting . . . intemperate
   b. ordaining . . . rectifying
   c. transmuting . . . inordinate
   d. dispersing . . . immutable
   e. tempering . . . penultimate

2. Adopting a male pseudonym and often appearing in men's attire, the French writer George Sand struck her fellow citizens as _____ but served as a(n) _____ of social equality for both men and women.
   a. inordinate . . . permutation
   b. temerarious . . . cosmopolite
   c. stellar . . . transmutation
   d. outré . . . apostle
   e. imperturbable . . . ultimatum

3. To be a "nosey Parker" means to be excessively meddlesome, as was a sixteenth-century Archbishop of Canterbury, Matthew Parker, whose fervid snooping into church business was considered both _____ and _____.
   a. temerarious . . . rectifying
   b. intemperate . . . perturbing
   c. immutable . . . temperate
   d. ordaining . . . epistolary
   e. turbid . . . insubordinate

4. Although two skaters collided in practice just before a world competition, in performance both displayed _____ in expression and dazzling _____ in their triple axles, drawing admiring applause.
   a. imperturbability . . . temerity
   b. ordinance . . . cosmology
   c. permutation . . . aspersion
   d. rectitude . . . dispersal
   e. temerity . . . rectitude

2 Circle the letter of the best answer.

1. Which root has no direct connection with matters "heavenly" or "universal order"?
   a. *kosmos*   b. *aster*   c. *ultra*   d. *ordo*   e. *stella*

2. Which root is "disorderly"?
   a. *regere*   b. *ordo*   c. *stella*   d. *temeritas*   e. *turbare*

3. outré : *ultimare* : :
   a. epistolary : *stellein*
   b. disperse : *mutare*
   c. temerarious : *temperare*
   d. turbid : *temere*
   e. *stella* : astral

4. stolid : fervor : :
   a. penultimate : ultimate
   b. righteous : rectitude
   c. temerarious : temerity
   d. cosmopolitan : urbanity
   e. imperturbable : perturbation

5. temerity : timid : :
   a. mutability : changeable
   b. enthusiasm : stolid
   c. ordinance : governed
   d. cosmos : universal
   e. aspersion : slanderous

6. *spargere* : to scatter : :
   a. *mutare* : to retain
   b. *turbare* : to calm
   c. *temperare* : to combine
   d. *ultimare* : to begin
   e. *stellein* : to dislocate

7. intemperate : control : :
   a. inordinate : appetite
   b. ordained : ultimatum
   c. temerarious : temperance
   d. outré : eccentricity
   e. immutable : dispersal

8. deliver : ultimatum : :
   a. ordain : epistle
   b. pontificate : temperance
   c. rectify : ordinance
   d. disperse : permutation
   e. cast : aspersion

9. cosmology : universe : :
   a. turbidity : opacity
   b. penultimate : ultimate
   c. hydrology : water
   d. ordination : religion
   e. apostle : epistle

10. insubordinate : *ordo* : :
   a. epistolary : *stella*
   b. cosmopolitan : *kosmos*
   c. stellar : *aster*
   d. turbid : *regere*
   e. perturbed : *temeritas*

3 Writing or Discussion Activities

1. As you read this list of sentence starters, find one that could apply to you. Expand the sentence to show what specific action or state of mind the word in bold-faced type expresses. If you can, follow the first sentence with two or three more sentences to complete the description of your experience.
   a. I was **perturbed** because . . .
   b. It's hard to **temper** one's feelings when . . .
   c. Mine was a **stellar** performance because . . .
   d. Although I don't like to be **insubordinate**, there are times when . . .
   e. I was surprised by my **temerity** when . . .

2. If you could be *transmuted* into some other form—animal, vegetable, or mineral—what would you be? Make a list of your new characteristics, physical and temperamental. Write a monologue in which you adopt a voice and point of view appropriate to your new self. Write about what you see around you every day with the eyes of your chosen creature or thing. Are you affable, caustic, credulous, ethereal, ignominious, inflammatory, loquacious, outré, sacrilegious, scintillating, or flamboyant? Exercise your sense of humor and irony.

3. Most people possess contradictory qualities. For example, a person can be indifferent about diet but be fervid to save dolphins and rain forests. As you look at the pairs of words below, apply them to yourself, and select a pair that works both ways for you. In a paragraph, provide at least two specific instances showing the opposites of feeling and behavior that coexist in your experience.
   a. temperate / intemperate
   b. cosmopolitan / unsophisticated
   c. inanimate / fervid
   d. outré / conservative
   e. stolid / scintillating
   If developing an imaginary character will give you more to write about, be inventive.

LESSONS 15 AND 16

Time

LESSON 15

Carpe diem.
Seize the day.—HORACE

Key Words		
anachronism	equinox	sojourn
annals	extempore	superannuated
biennial	meridian	synchronous
chronicle	millennium	temporal
diurnal	nocturne	temporize

TEMPUS, TEMPORIS <L. "time"

Familiar Words
contemporary
tempo
temporary

Challenge Words
contemporize
O tempore! O mores!

1. **extempore** (ĕk stĕm´ pə rē, ĭk stĕm´ pə rə)
   [*ex* <L. "from," "out of"]
   adj. Improvised; composed or uttered without advance preparation.

   Politicians who deviate from a prepared text have sometimes regretted their **extempore** remarks.

   adv. Without advance preparation.

   Using topics suggested by fellow students, the improvisation class performed **extempore** a skit about football and fishing.

   extemporaneous, *adj.*; **extemporary**, *adj.*; **extemporize**, *v.*

2. temporal (tĕm´ pər əl, tem´ prəl)
adj. 1. Pertaining to worldly affairs.

St. Paul in his Epistle to the Corinthians writes, "The things which are seen are **temporal**; but the things which are unseen are eternal."

2. Transitory; short-lived.

With new technology, biologists can study closeups of **temporal** changes in the life of each cell.

NOTA BENE: The word *temporal* sometimes serves in a different context, as in the phrase, "the *temporal* bones of the skull."

3. temporize (tĕm´ pə rīz)
intr. v. 1. To accept or adapt to a situation; to compromise.

At the end of Elizabeth Bowen's novel *The Death of the Heart*, young Portia forces her cool, insensitive guardians to **temporize** with her before she will agree to rejoin them.

2. To postpone a decision in order to gain time.

Believing that his Army of the Potomac needed more training and equipment, Civil War Commander George B. McClellan **temporized** too long and lost the Peninsular Campaign designed to capture Richmond.

KHRONOS <G. "time"

<table>
<tr><td>

Familiar Words
chronic
chronology
crony

</td></tr>
</table>

4. anachronism (ə năk´ rə nĭz´ əm)
[*ana* <G. "up"]
n. 1. A person or thing out of place in a historical period or sequence of events.

Serious historical novelists check facts to avoid **anachronisms**: only by the nineteenth century can characters forsake quill pens and inkwells for typewriters.

2. A person, custom, or idea considered out-of-date.

In order to preserve simplicity in their lives, the Amish consciously choose the **anachronism** of the horse-drawn buggy rather than the automobile.

anachronistic, *adj.*

<table>
<tr><td>

Challenge Words
chronaxy
chronogram
chronograph
chronometer
chronometry
chronoscope

</td></tr>
</table>

5. chronicle (krŏn´ ĭ kəl)
n. A continuous, detailed record of historical events in order of their occurrence.
(When capitalized, Chronicles I and II in the Old Testament.)

J.R.R. Tolkien's trilogy, *The Lord of the Rings*, is a **chronicle** of the great war between the hobbits, who possess the One Ring, and the Enemy, who have corrupted it with their evil power.

chronicle, *v.*; **chronicler,** *n.*

6. **synchronous** (sĭn´ krə nəs, sĭng´ krə nəs) [*syn* = *sun* <G. "same"] *adj.* Happening at the same time; moving at the same rate.

Castor and Pollux, known as the Gemini, are like many other astral twins: **synchronous** in their movement through space even though a quarter of a light year apart.

synchronistic, *adj.*; **synchronize,** *v.*; **synchrony,** *n.*

ANNUS <L. "year"

<table>
<tr><td>

Familiar Words
annalist
anniversary
annual

</td></tr>
</table>

<table>
<tr><td>

Challenge Words
annuity
decennium
quadrennium
quinquennium
vicennial

</td></tr>
</table>

7. **annals** (ăn´ əlz) *n.* (plural) 1. A chronological record of events of successive years without interpretation or analysis by the author; a historical record.

Opera buffs can often be found perusing The ***Annals** of the Metropolitan Opera: The Complete Chronicle of Performances and Artists.*

2. A periodical journal of a learned field or annual reports of an organization.

The **annals** of the Audubon Society can inform you of their yearly progress in preserving and studying wildlife.

NOTA BENE: When you investigate actual *chronicles* and *annals* you will discover that the terms may overlap: *annals* sometimes applies to history, or is used synonymously, as in the Metropolitan Opera *Annals*, with *chronicles*. However, chroniclers will be more likely than annalists to refer to themselves in their historical accounts and to analyze events in their own or past time.

8. **biennial** (bī ĕn´ ē əl) [*bi* <L. "two"] *adj.* 1. Lasting two years.

The hollyhock is a **biennial** plant, flowering only in the second year of its two-year cycle in most climates.

2. Happening every two years.

The **biennial** arts festival in Venice, the *Biennale*, draws performers and visitors from around the world.

biennial, *n.*; **biennially,** *adv.*

NOTA BENE: Don't confuse *biennial* with *biannual*, which means "semiannual" or "happening twice each year," as in "Horse-lovers swarm to the *biannual* steeplechase held in April and September."

9. **millennium**   (mə lĕn´ ē əm; plural **millennia**, **millenniums**)
[*mille* <L. "thousand"]
n. 1. A span of one thousand years.

Scientists have determined that the separation of North America from Africa 180 **millennia** ago made way for the formation of the Atlantic Ocean.

2. The thousand years during which Christ is to rule on earth; any anticipated period of peace, justice, and joy.

The Church of Jesus Christ of Latter-Day Saints conveys in its name the basic tenet of Mormon faith: that we are living in the last days before the coming of the **millennium**.

millenarian, *adj.*; **millenary**, *adj.*; **millennial**, *adj.*

10. **superannuated**   (soo´ pər ăn´ yoo ā´ təd)   [*super* <L. "above"]
adj. 1. Retired or disqualified because of age or infirmity.

Despite her age, Mother Teresa has resisted **superannuated** status because the demands of her work with the young, the ill, and the homeless are never ending.

2. Antiquated; obsolete.

"There is not a more unhappy being than a **superannuated** idol."—Joseph Addison

superannuate, *v.*; **superannuation**, *n.*

DIES <L. "day"

11. **diurnal**   (dī ûr´ nəl)
adj. 1. Daily; occurring in a day or every day.

In "Contemplations" Anne Bradstreet reflects on the power of the sun and its "swift annual and **diurnal** course," the former giving us seasons, the latter, day and night.

2. Active during the daytime rather than at night.

Because bees rely on the sun to navigate, their work of gathering nectar is always **diurnal**.

12. **meridian**   (mə rĭd´ ē ən)   [*meri* = *medius* <L. "mid," "middle"]
n. 1. The highest point or stage of development; apogee; zenith.

In the 1920s a constellation of African-American writers reached a **meridian** now known as the Harlem Renaissance.

Familiar Words
dial
diary
diet
dismal
journal
journey

Challenge Words
circadian
Dies Irae
dies non juridicus
quotidian
sine die

2. The imaginary half circle connecting the North and South poles.

Think of the **meridians** as resembling the curved indentations on a pumpkin.

meridional, *adj.*

NOTA BENE: The familiar abbreviations A.M. and P.M. to indicate times before and after noon stand for *ante meridiem,* "before noon," and *post meridiem,* "after noon."

13. **sojourn** (sō´ jûrn, sō jûrn´)
[*so = sub* <L. "under"]
n. A temporary stay; a brief visit.

Although Charlotte Brontë's **sojourn** in Brussels was a period of intense loneliness, it provided her with the material for her novel *Villette.*

intr. v. To stay for a time; to reside temporarily.

Before his final exile on the island of Saint Helena, Napoleon had **sojourned** on the isle of Elba.

NOTA BENE: Also derived from *dies* is the word *quotidian,* which means "daily," but also carries the connotation of "commonplace": "Wearied by her *quotidian* routine, the typesetter used her time off to sojourn in Hawaii."

Challenge Words
noctambulation
noctilucent
noctuid

NOX, NOCTIS <L. "night"

14. **nocturne** (nŏk´ tûrn´)
n. A melody or composition conveying romantic or evening thoughts; a reverie.

The Polish pianist and composer Frederic Chopin composed nineteen **nocturnes.**

nocturnal, *adj.*

15. **equinox** (ē´ kwə nŏks, ĕk´ wə nŏks) [*equi* <L. "equal"]
n. Each of the two times of the year when days and nights are of equal length.

The two **equinoxes** fall on March 21 and September 23.

equinoctial, *adj.*

EXERCISE 15A Circle the letter of the best SYNONYM for the word in bold-faced type.

1. the **meridian** of Pavlova's fame a. apogee b. midpoint
   c. promontory d. lowest point e. hyperbole
2. **superannuated** machinery a. high-powered b. automatic
   c. latest-model d. weathered e. antiquated
3. lasted a(n) **millennium** a. period of two years b. lifetime
   c. thousand years d. evening e. hundred years
4. a speech delivered **extempore** a. well-rehearsed b. unprepared
   c. unannounced d. fervidly e. dispiritedly
5. **chronicles** from the days of whaling ships a. ships' logs
   b. diaries c. clocks d. biographies e. chronological accounts of
   events

Circle the letter of the best ANTONYM for the word in bold-faced type.

6. **synchronous** movements a. simultaneous b. well-timed
   c. dissimilar d. out-of-step e. confluent
7. **temporal** truths a. clocked b. superannuated c. brief
   d. intemperate e. eternal
8. a tendency to **temporize** a. procrastinate b. reflect
   c. rush ahead d. overeat e. pacify
9. to **sojourn** in the mountains a. rusticate b. dwell for a long time
   c. travel d. camp e. temporize
10. **nocturnal** sounds a. nightly b. mysterious c. daily
    d. daytime e. perennial

EXERCISE 15B Circle the letter of the sentence in which the word in bold-faced type is
used incorrectly.

1. a. At its **meridian**, from 1500 to 1200 B.C., the culture of Crete and
      Mycenae dominated the Mediterranean.
   b. Longitude is measured from the prime **meridian** at Greenwich
      near London.
   c. "A snake's belt slips because it has no hips" is a jingle underscoring
      the fact that a snake lacks a **meridian**.
   d. In describing kinds of apples, Henry David Thoreau likens "the
      fine blood-red rays running regularly from the stem-dimple to
      the blossoming end" to **meridional** lines.
2. a. A species of **diurnal** burrowing owls lives by the city dump.
   b. According to the travelers' **diurnals**, the sojourn in Australia was
      the meridian of their trip.
   c. Sleep releases us from **diurnal** care.
   d. Some flowers, like tulips and morning glories, open their petals
      diurnally but close them nocturnally.

3. a. Parents learn that the temper tantrums of the "terrible twos" are expected of **biennial** babies.

   b. Because board members need to meet more often, they changed their schedule from **biennial** to biannual meetings.

   c. Congressional elections are held **biennially**.

   d. Foxglove and parsley are **biennials**, needing to be resown every two years.

4. a. A **superannuated** employee may miss regular work at first but eventually like the new freedom.

   b. Because the rebellious Kate **superannuates** her younger sister and is expected to marry first, sweet-tempered Bianca is grateful to the successful suitor in *The Taming of the Shrew*.

   c. Jet planes have almost entirely **superannuated** Atlantic luxury liners.

   d. How can I write a paper on this **superannuated** typewriter when I'm accustomed to a word processor?

5. a. Snowbound for weeks in the Sierra, members of the Donner Party **temporized** with conscience before accepting cannibalism as their only means of survival.

   b. Pressed to grant a later curfew, parents may **temporize** before making a decision.

   c. When Scarlett O'Hara cannot bear to think about the future, she **temporizes** by saying, "Tomorrow's another day."

   d. Recent technology has produced fabrics that **temporize** comfort in any climate.

6. a. The dressmaker acknowledged her **anachronistic** preference for an old treadle sewing machine rather than for a new electronic model.

   b. In the title role of the film *Cleopatra*, Elizabeth Taylor rides under an **anachronistic** Roman arch not built until thirty years after the death of that Egyptian queen.

   c. Although the DC-3 is an **anachronism** alongside jet aircraft, renovated or rebuilt versions of that old plane still fly.

   d. Appearing at a fancy dinner in scruffy jeans and a tee shirt is a discourteous **anachronism** to one's hosts.

7. a. Tenth-century Welsh **annals** known as *Annabules Cambriae* mention a battle in which Arthur dies, furnishing one of the sources of the legend of King Arthur.

   b. Mary Chestnut **annals** a personal record of the Civil War years on a plantation in South Carolina.

   c. In **annals** about the Roman people, the historian Livy describes the war that Hannibal of Carthage waged in Italy, with massive armies and thirty-seven elephants.

   d. The **annals** of the Royal Society, founded in 1662, crowd library shelves with reports of growth of the physical sciences.

8. a. Those who believe in life after death can accept **temporal** setbacks because they anticipate a peaceful future in the next life.
   b. Joy may be **temporal**, Willa Cather seems to say in "Rose-time": "Oh, this is the joy of the rose; / That it blows / And goes."
   c. Although the mediators were calm and **temporal**, the session exploded with unsolved problems.
   d. People suffering from chronic diseases like diabetes welcome the **temporal** relief that insulin gives them.

EXERCISE 15C   Fill in each blank with the most appropriate word from Lesson 15. Use a word or any of its forms only once.

1. Katherine Mansfield's _____ in Bavaria provided material for her stories *In a German Pension*.

2. More than three and one-half _____ ago China's written records and bronze vessels marked the advancement of its civilization.

3. The striking clock in Act 2 of Shakespeare's *Julius Caesar* is a famous _____.

4. In Bernal Díaz's _____, *The True History of New Spain*, he reports events as he experiences them, including the death of Montezuma, king of Mexico.

5. When interviewed on television, the comic Robin Williams amazes his audience with spontaneous, _____ characterizations and sound effects.

6. The author of *Dibs: In Search of Self* writes that the darkening of the _____ sky "gives growing room for softened judgments, for suspended indictments, for emotional hospitality."

7. Makers of the film *Gone with the Wind* overlooked that in a hospital scene the shadows on the wall were not _____ with the movements of the actors.

8. We take for granted the _____ progress of the sun from rising to setting.

9. Because the flea market requires more preparation every year, the organizers now hold it _____ rather than annually.

10. As early as 140 B.C. Hipparchos of Nicaea had figured out the astronomical irregularities in the rotation of the planets that affect the _____ occurring twice each year.

11. Expand your knowledge of American history with *Treasury of Anecdotes, Epigrams, and Puns; Nuggets of Historical Debate and Gems*

of *Eloquence All Handpicked from the* _____
of Congress, 1789 to the Present (1961).

12. Known for her epigrams, the film actress Mae West advised against

_____ when she said, "He who hesitates is last."

EXERCISE 15D   Replace the word or phrase in italics with a key word (or any of its forms) from Lesson 15.

On New Year's Eve of the year 2000, seniors at Cosmopolitan High School are planning to celebrate a rare occasion: a graduation year that links two (1) *thousand-year periods.** Students are writing a humorous review, (2) *"Night-piece* for a Millennium," which invites stellar figures from the second millennium for a (3) *brief visit* on the stage at CHS. First among these (4) *chronologically erroneous* guests is Leonardo da Vinci, who will give a(n) (5) *on-the-spot* analysis of avant-garde paintings and drawings by senior art students. Next Lady Murasaki will be gratified to learn from literature students that even nine centuries after its publication her novel, *The Tale of Genji*, has escaped (6) *the condition of being an outmoded relic.*

Copernicus and Galileo will rejoice that their lives are (7) *happening at the same time* for a few hours, and they will admire models of the spacecraft (8) *Apogee*, which student designers predict will take cruises (9) *every two years* to Venus. When Karl Marx enters, he will scowl and shake his fist, unwilling to (10) *compromise* his faith in Communism despite its collapse in many parts of the world. On December 31, 2000, these and other visitors will celebrate the confluence of centuries and millennia.

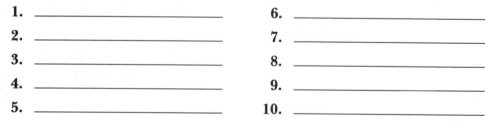

1. _____   6. _____

2. _____   7. _____

3. _____   8. _____

4. _____   9. _____

5. _____   10. _____

_____

*A new century begins officially with a 1, not a 0.

LESSON 16

Senectus est natura loquacior.
Old age is by nature more talkative.—CICERO

	Key Words	
demur	memorabilia	nova
dour	moratorium	novice
duress	neoclassical	obdurate
immemorial	neologism	senescent
memoir	neophyte	surly

Familiar Words
innovation
novel
novelette
novelist
novelty
renovate

NOVUS <L. "new"

1. nova (nō´ və)
n. A star that increases thousands of times in brightness and then fades.

Although a longtime resident of the heavens, a **nova** becomes "new" when it blazes into brilliance for days, weeks, or months and then grows dim again.

Challenge Words
art nouveau
nouveau riche
novella
novelistic
novitiate
supernova

2. novice (nŏv´ ĭs)
n. A person new to any field; a beginner.

In fields like ice skating, carpentry, or mountain climbing, a **novice** can expect an injury or two, disappointment, and hard work before mastery sets in.

Familiar Word
neon

NEOS <G. "new"

3. neoclassical (nē´ ō klăs´ ə kəl) [*classicus* <L. "of the first rank" in ancient Rome]
n. A revival of literary, architectural, musical, and artistic forms that are considered a standard or model, and therefore "classical."

Challenge Words
neocosmic
Neo-Darwinism
neogenesis
neolithic
Neoplatonism

Between 1775 and 1850 American enthusiasm for Greek and Roman architecture was expressed in the construction of **neoclassical** banks and libraries across the country.

neoclassicism, *n.*

NOTA BENE: Although applying to a revival of something admired in a variety of arts and cultures, *neoclassical* also has more specific meanings. It often refers to the admiration of ancient Greek and Roman art and literature in England and Europe. English writers in the seventeenth and eighteenth centuries became critical of unrestrained emotion and imagination, placing emphasis on reason and common sense associated with Greek writers and philosophers. English and European architecture between 1775 and 1850 began to show the influence of Greek temples and other structures revealed through archaeological excavation. During this period *neoclassical* architecture, in reaction against baroque and rococo ornamentation, adopted columns and domes characteristic of Greek and Roman buildings.

4. neologism   (nē ŏl´ ə jĭz əm)   [*logos* <G. "word," "study"]
n. A new word, phrase, or expression, or a new meaning for an old word.

As cosmologists go deeper into the universe, they develop **neologisms** for new concepts, words like *quasar,* a contraction of "quasi-stellar," and give new meaning to familiar words, like *big bang.*

5. neophyte   (nē´ ə fīt)   [*phutos* <G. "grown"]
n. 1. A recent convert.

Although for many years he was a dedicated "Black Muslim," on his pilgrimage to Mecca Malcolm X learned he was a mere **neophyte**, a newcomer to Islamic tradition, not even knowing how to pray.

2. A newly ordained priest or member of a religious order.

A **neophyte** in the order of the Poor Clares wears a rope belt with three knots to signify completion of the first stage as a novice.

3. A beginner; a novice.

Even as **neophytes** on the tennis circuit, Chris Evert and Martina Navratilova displayed the agility and finesse of champions.

<table>
<tr><td>

Familiar Words
durable
duration
during
endure
</td></tr>
</table>

DURO, DURARE, DURAVI, DURATUM <L. "to make hard," "to endure"

6. dour   (do͝or, dour)
adj. Stern; grim; gloomy.

In *Silas Marner* a **dour** misanthrope gradually thaws as an orphaned child opens her heart to him.

7. duress (do͞o rĕs´, dyo͞o rĕs´, do͝or´ ĭs, dyo͝or´ ĭs)
n. Forced constraint; coercion against one's will.

News of hostages held under **duress** reached their families only sporadically as other hostages were released.

8. obdurate (ŏb´ dyo͞o rĭt, ŏb´ do͞o rət)
[*ob* <L. "off," "against"]
adj. 1. Stubborn; unyielding.

Justifiably **obdurate**, Betsey Trotwood refuses to let a cold, neglectful stepfather claim guardianship of her orphaned nephew, David Copperfield.

2. Hardened against good influence; impenitent.

No James Bond thriller is without an **obdurate** enemy whom Bond can demolish in a dramatic climax.

obduracy, *n.*

MEMORIA <L. "remembrance," "memory"

9. immemorial (ĭm´ ə môr´ ē əl,
ĭm´ ə mōr´ ē əl) [*im = in* <L. "not"]
adj. Going deep into the past before history, knowledge, or memory; primordial.

Ice cores in Antarctica allow scientists to study the fluctuations in climate from an **immemorial** period dating back more than 160,000 years.

10. memoir (mĕm´ wär´, mĕm´ wôr´)
n. (usually plural) A written account of events one has lived through; an autobiography.

Simone de Beauvoir's ***Memoirs*** of a *Dutiful Daughter* recounts the joys and uncertainties of her first twenty years.

11. memorabilia (mĕm´ ər ə bĭl´ ē ə,
mĕm´ ər ə bĭl´ yə)
n. Things worthy of remembrance.

Collectors of **memorabilia** prize Elvis Presley's comb or a pair of ruby slippers worn by Judy Garland in *The Wizard of Oz*.

Challenge Word
moratory

MOROR, MORARI, MORATUM <L. "to delay," "to loiter," "to tarry"

12. demur (dĭ mûr´) [*de* <L. "away from"]
intr. v. 1. To raise an objection.

It is permissible to **demur** when you are asked impertinent questions.

2. To delay.

Before sending an acceptance letter to a college, students often **demur** until they have visited the campus.

demur, *n.*; **demurral**, *n.*

13. moratorium (môr´ ə tôr´ ē əm, môr´ ə tōr´ ē əm, mŏr´ ə tōr´ ē əm; plural **moratoriums** or **moratoria**)
n. Deferment or delay of any action.

In the worst days of the Great Depression in the 1930s, banks declared a "bank holiday," a **moratorium** on payments in order to give themselves time to replenish funds.

Familiar Words
senate
senile
senior
sir

SENEX, SENIS <L. "old," "an elder"
SENESCO, SENESCERE, SENUI <L. "to grow old"

14. senescent (sĭ nĕs´ ənt)
adj. Growing old; aging.

Senescent Lucinda Matlock in *Spoon River Anthology* accepts at her death her ninety-six years, seventy years of marriage, and twelve children.

senescence, *n.*

Challenge Words
seignior
senectitude
señor
señora
sire

15. surly (sûr´ lē)
adj. Flagrantly uncivil and ill-natured.

After bequeathing his territories to them, King Lear cannot believe that his daughters Goneril and Regan have turned **surly**, refusing his royal retainers and shutting their gates against him.

surliness, *n.*

EXERCISE 16A

Circle the letter of the best SYNONYM for the word in bold-faced type.

1. despite their **demur**   a. clamor   b. objection   c. duress
d. acceptance   e. temerity

2. an inventor of **neologisms**   a. anagrams   b. logical theories
   c. superannuated dogma   d. theorems   e. new words
3. the exhumed **memoirs**   a. memories   b. biography
   c. historical documents   d. autobiography   e. volumes of poetry
4. facing hardships as **neophytes**   a. converts   b. visitors
   c. old-timers   d. inventors   e. boxers
5. discovering a(n) **nova**   a. constellation   b. asteroid   c. comet
   d. brilliant star   e. supernova
6. **neoclassicism** in music   a. innovation   b. superannuation
   c. adaptation of an admired model   d. popular style
   e. anachronism
7. their **dour** captain   a. stingy   b. stern   c. superannuated
   d. jovial   e. indulgent

Circle the letter of the best ANTONYM for the word in bold-faced type.

8. an unexpected **moratorium**   a. review   b. obituary
   c. acceleration   d. sojourn   e. delay
9. the loser's **surly** reply   a. temerarious   b. respectful   c. rude
   d. caustic   e. indifferent
10. despite **duress**   a. difficulty   b. independence   c. hardness
    d. restraint   e. freedom
11. the **obdurate** store manager   a. hardhearted   b. unyielding
    c. stubborn   d. greedy   e. yielding
12. a **novice** at the helm   a. newcomer   b. sailor   c. veteran
    d. numbskull   e. beginner
13. a model of hearty **senescence**   a. youth   b. ill health
    c. superannuation   d. maturity   e. bad judgment
14. famous explorers' **memorabilia**   a. photographs   b. dirt samples
    c. meaningless trifles   d. treasured possessions   e. diaries
15. **immemorial** traces of life   a. historical   b. primordial
    c. forgotten   d. futuristic   e. remembered

EXERCISE 16B   Circle the letter of the sentence in which the word in bold-faced type is used incorrectly.

1. a. Monastic **neophytes** received the tonsure, a haircut with the crown of the head shaved.
   b. Tapped at age seventeen to replace the prima ballerina of Britain's Royal Ballet, the **neophyte** Margot Fonteyn began a stellar career that lasted more than fifty years.
   c. As a **neophyte** rabbi, she is eager to learn more Hebrew.
   d. Are you going to buy **neophytes** to replace your worn-out running shoes?

2. a. If friends press you to run for a school office and you say "I'll sleep on it," or "I'll let the idea hang fire for a day or two," you're **demurring**.

b. When her grandmother finds Janie a husband, she **demurs**, but then in her innocence accepts him, to her sorrow as the reader learns in Zora Neale Hurston's novel *Their Eyes Were Watching God*.

c. Some people will swallow a camel but **demur** at a gnat.

d. Despite her **demur** appearance, she eagerly entered the triathlon competition.

3. a. The **neologism**, "jeans," was introduced by Levi Strauss in 1853 when he responded to miners' need for durable clothing by adapting the blue canvas pants worn by Genovese sailors.

b. When Benoit Mandelbrot needed a name for structured irregularities in nature, he coined the word *fractals*, a **neologism** from Latin *frangere*, meaning "to break."

c. Students sometimes commit **neologisms** in wrong spelling: "mispell" and "recurence" for the correct *misspell* and *recurrence*.

d. "Mondegreen" is a **neologism** for a misinterpretation of what is heard; lines from a Scottish ballad, "They hae slay the Earl of Murray, / And hae laid him on the green," were heard as "They hae slay the Earl of Murray, / And Lady Mondegreen."

4. a. The novice skiers were in trouble when a sudden blizzard obscured their tracks and made visibility **obdurate**.

b. Among animals, the mule is the symbol of **obduracy**.

c. To remain **obdurate** in the face of inevitable defeat, even for a worthy cause, can be costly to reputation as well as to the pocketbook.

d. With her characterization of the **obdurate** overseer of slaves, Simon Legree, Harriet Beecher Stowe made her novel *Uncle Tom's Cabin* an incendiary antislavery tract.

EXERCISE 16C   Fill in each blank with the most appropriate word from Lesson 16. Use a word or any of its forms only once.

1. Celebrated auction houses like Sotheby's and Christie's obtain high prices for noteworthy discarded _____ of famous persons.

2. The taped _____ of Nate Shaw, an illiterate slave, document his gifts as storyteller and survivor of hardship and racial prejudice.

3. Mothers of Chileans who were held under _____ and disappeared following the 1973 coup have sought help through genetic research to identify and match the recovered remains with surviving grandchildren.

4. Adapting ancestral designs of pots exhumed in the 1890s, the Hopi craftswoman Nampeyo developed a(n) _____ style of pottery equaling the elegance of earlier works.

5. A(n) _____ on aerosols because of their harmful effect on the ozone layer has forced manufacturing changes.

6. Like a(n) _____, in the 1930s Soviet agronomist Trofim Lysenko blazed into prominence with his Marxist wheat-growing theories, only to fall into disgrace when they proved to be wholly untenable.

7. The most remarkable example of _____ in the Bible is Methuselah, who is said to have lived to be 969 years old.

8. Fossils of cockroaches prove that they have abounded from time _____.

9. As young Pip lingers beside family gravestones, a man arises from the mist, _____ and terrifying: "Keep still, you little devil, or I'll cut your throat!"

10. In the novel *One Flew over the Cuckoo's Nest,* patients in the mental hospital do their best to outwit the _____ and rigid Nurse Ratchett.

11. Starting at age nine as a(n) _____, Rose Bertin learned the craft of dressmaking well and became the unofficial "minister" of eighteenth-century French fashion, especially of hats.

EXERCISE 16D   Among the four choices in the parentheses, circle the word that best fits the context.

A. The U.S. Park Service requests visitors to "leave only footprints; take only pictures." Even bringing home rocks or acorns as (1. memoirs / moratoriums / memorabilia / chronicles) of a camping trip is forbidden. Although nature lovers appreciate this effort to preserve the (2. immemorial / neoclassical / obdurate / senescent) beauty of the wilderness, some campers are (3. dour / obdurate / senescent / surly), resisting requests not to gather wildflowers or collect shells whenever they wish in "their" park.

B. Despite an official moratorium, the West Point tradition of hazing (4. immemorial / demurring / neophyte / senescent) cadets during their freshman year has continued. Senior cadets subject these (5. neologisms / novices / novas / obdurates) to many forms of (6. demur / memoirs / moratoria / duress) to test obedience and self-discipline in the face of insults and humiliation.

C. Thrushcross Grange, the elegant manor house of the Linton family, contrasts sharply with Wuthering Heights, the Earnshaws' rough stone farmhouse. The inhabitants of Wuthering Heights are severe and (7. dour / senescent / obdurate / surly), even (8. dour / senescent / obdurate / surly), treating strangers with suspicion and rudeness. Heathcliff, the relentless master of Wuthering Heights, cannot forgive indignities suffered from his adoptive family and the marriage of his love, Catherine, to a Linton. He is (9. dour / senescent / obdurate / surly) in holding young Catherine Linton captive until she marries his invalid son. This classic tale of love and vengeance is narrated by Nelly Dean, the (10. dour / senescent / obdurate / surly) and sympathetic housekeeper who has come to know intimately three generations of both families in her long years of service.

REVIEW EXERCISES FOR LESSONS 15 AND 16

1 Circle the letter of the best answer.

1. Which of the following words has nothing "new" in it?
a. nova   b. neoclassical   c. moratorium   d. novice   e. neophyte

2. Which of the following words contains no "time"?
a. synchronous   b. temporal   c. chronicle   d. duress   e. extempore

3. Which of the following words contains no "year"?
a. biennial   b. meridian   c. superannuated   d. annals
e. millennium

4. Which of the following words contains no "day"?
a. sojourn   b. diurnal   c. quotidian   d. equinox   e. meridian

5. *novus : neos* : :
a. *memoria : morari*
b. *tempus : khronos*
c. *durus : annus*
d. *memoria : senex*
e. *dies : nox*

6. temporal : spiritual : :
   a. surly : equinoctial
   b. obdurate : sinning
   c. diurnal : nocturnal
   d. extempore : neologistic
   e. dour : immemorial

7. chronicle : history : :
   a. memoir : autobiography
   b. neoclassicism : architecture
   c. anachronism : error
   d. memorabilia : objects
   e. annals : organization

2 Matching: On the line at the left, write the letter of the phrase that most accurately defines the pairs of words.

_____ **1.** a *senescent nova*

_____ **2.** a *dour novice*

_____ **3.** an *extempore nocturne*

_____ **4.** a *moratorium* on *memorabilia*

_____ **5.** *temporal duress*

_____ **6.** *immemorial millennia*

_____ **7.** a *temporizing neophyte*

_____ **8.** a *surly demur*

_____ **9.** *synchronous memoirs*

_____ **10.** *anachronistic neoclassicisms*

_____ **11.** an *obdurate chronicler*

_____ **12.** a *diurnal neologism*

A. primordial thousands-of-years
B. perfectly matched autobiographies
C. a hold on [a collection of] treasured objects
D. historically incorrect adaptations of Greek art
E. an aging star of faded brilliance
F. a compromising convert
G. a glum beginner
H. a stubborn historian
I. a new word every day
J. an impromptu poem about night
K. a sullen objection
L. temporary restraint

3 Writing or Discussion Activities

1. When have you been a *novice*? Recall the way you felt when you first began something, for example, playing baseball or chess, cooking, using a computer, babysitting, or working as a salesperson. In a paragraph, write about your reactions through the steps of the learning process, acquiring skills and confidence in a new activity. Tell about your struggles and successes. Include a comment about the lasting effect of the experience of being a learner, now that you are no longer a neophyte.

2. Have you been the owner of *superannuated memorabilia*—cherished possessions that have outlived their function or appeal for you? Think of an object that once meant much but now means little, and perhaps has been discarded: childhood toys, collections of like objects, a family heirloom, or an obsolete gadget replaced by a newer model. Describe the object at the height of its value for you, and explain its loss of functional or emotional importance. Let your description of the object and its subsequent superannuation be clear to the reader.

3. To *temporize* can mean "to compromise" or "to come to terms" with someone or something. In both life and literature, people face situations requiring adjustment, whether they are willing or not. Choose a person real or fictional who has had to temporize with a power or personality demanding adjustment in thought, attitude, and even a way of life. Write a paragraph explaining the situation needing change, the attitude of the temporizing person toward that change, and the extent of benefit or harm brought about by the compromise.

WORD LIST

(Numbers in parentheses refer to the lesson in which the word appears.)

acclamation (8)
accredit (1)
acronym (5)
affable (7)
agnostic (3)
alliteration (5)
amnesty (3)
anachronism (15)
analogy (6)
animus (10)
annals (15)
apogee (9)
apologist (6)
apostle (13)
apotheosis (1)
arraign (3)
ascribe (5)
aspersion (14)
aspiration (10)
asterisk (13)
astral (13)
atheist (1)

biennial (15)

caustic (11)
cauterize (11)
choreography (6)
chronicle (15)
circumlocution (8)
circumscribe (5)

clamor (8)
cognition (4)
cognizant (4)
colloquium (8)
compute (4)
conflagration (11)
confluence (12)
connoisseur (4)
conscientious (4)
conscription (5)
consecrate (2)
constellation (13)
cormorant (12)
cosmology (13)
cosmopolite (13)
credence (1)
creditable (1)
credulous (1)
creed (1)
criterion (3)

declaim (8)
dehydrate (12)
deify (1)
deity (1)
demur (16)
diaphanous (10)
dictatorial (7)
diction (7)
dictum (7)
disperse (14)

dispirited (10)
ditty (7)
diurnal (15)
divine (1)
divinity (1)
dogma (3)
dogmatic (3)
dour (16)
duress (16)

eclectic (6)
edict (7)
effervescent (11)
effluent (12)
epigram (6)
epigraph (6)
epilogue (6)
epiphany (10)
epistolary (13)
equanimity (10)
equinox (15)
ether (10)
ethereal (10)
eulogy (6)
execrate (2)
exhume (9)
expiate (2)
extempore (15)

fervid (11)
flagrant (11)

flamboyant (11)
flux (12)
forensic (8)
forum (8)
frenetic (3)

geocentric (9)
gloss (7)
graffiti (6)
graphic (6)

heterodox (3)
hierarchy (2)
hieroglyphic (2)
humus (9)
hydrology (12)
hyperbole (10)
hyperborean (10)
hyperventilation (10)
hypocrisy (3)

ignominious (5)
immemorial (16)
immutable (14)
impious (2)
imperturbable (14)
impute (4)
incendiary (11)
incense (11)
indict (7)
indite (7)

ineffable (7)

inflammatory (11)

inordinate (13)

insubordinate (13)

inter (9)

interdiction (7)

inundate (12)

jurisdiction (7)

lexicon (6)

lingo (8)

lingua franca (8)

linguist (8)

literal (5)

literate (5)

lithograph (6)

locution (8)

logistics (6)

logo (6)

loquacious (8)

malediction (7)

marinade (12)

memoir (16)

memorabilia (16)

meridian (15)

millennium (15)

mnemonic (3)

moratorium (16)

mountebank (9)

nauseate (12)

nave (12)

neoclassical (16)

neologism (16)

neophyte (16)

nocturne (15)

nomenclature (5)

notorious (4)

nova (16)

novice (16)

obdurate (16)

obliterate (5)

onomatopoeia (5)

ordain (13)

ordinance (13)

outré (14)

pantheism (1)

pantheon (1)

paramount (9)

pastoral (9)

penultimate (14)

perigee (9)

permutation (14)

perturb (14)

phantasm (10)

physiognomy (3)

piety (2)

pittance (2)

plebiscite (4)

polyglot (7)

pontiff (12)

pontificate (12)

presage (4)

prescience (4)

prognosis (3)

promontory (9)

proscribe (5)

proverbial (8)

pseudonym (5)

pusillanimous (10)

putative (4)

pyre (11)

pyromania (11)

pyrotechnics (11)

rationale (3)

rationalize (3)

rectify (13)

rectitude (13)

redound (12)

redundant (12)

repast (9)

repute (4)

rustic (9)

rusticate (9)

sacrament (2)

sacrilege (2)

sacrosanct (2)

sagacious (4)

sage (4)

sanctimonious (2)

sanction (2)

sanctity (2)

sanctuary (2)

sapient (4)

schizophrenia (3)

scintilla (11)

scintillate (11)

senescent (16)

sojourn (15)

stellar (13)

stolid (13)

subscribe (5)

superannuated (15)

surly (16)

sycophant (10)

synchronous (15)

temerarious (14)

temerity (14)

temper (14)

temperance (14)

temporal (15)

temporize (15)

terra cotta (9)

terrestrial (9)

theocracy (1)

theology (1)

topography (6)

transcribe (5)

transmute (14)

turbid (14)

ultimatum (14)

undulate (12)

valediction (7)

vent (10)

verbatim (8)

verbose (8)